Introduction

For Teacher:

Table Toppers 3 teaches and reinforces the basic **Multipli...**
while challenging the pupil to remember and apply what has been learned
through daily activities and weekly tests.

How to use this book:

- **Learn**   Do one unit each week (**Day 1** on Monday, **Day 2** on Tuesday,
  Day 3 on Wednesday and **Day 4** on Thursday).

- **Test**   Friday is **Test Day**. The last line on **Day 4** of each unit directs the
  child to the **Test** page e.g. — '**Do Test 1 on page 58.**'
  Pupils record their **Test Scores** on **page 76**.

- **Revision**   These are **Revision** units in order to revise, consolidate and
  evaluate progress. Pupils record their **Revision Scores** on **page 77**.

The Seventy Fivers (at the end of the book) provide end-of-year testing of tables.

Tips!

- The relevant table should be recited daily.

- The secret of teaching tables is to keep it short and sharp, and repeat every day!
  Each day's work should take approximately 10 minutes.

- *Table Toppers* is success-based. Less confident children can find all the answers
  needed at the top of each page in the table box. This allows pupils of every
  ability to achieve a high level of correct answers. As pupils' proficiency grows,
  they will no longer need to refer to these answers.

- The tables are not presented in numerical sequence. Instead, they are ordered
  according to 'difficulty' (e.g. beginning with **10s** which are clearly the easiest
  tables to learn). For this reason the units should be taught as presented.

- Where an answer to a sum is provided as an example, it is not to be included
  in the pupil's score.

- Links to **Tables Games** and IT/IWB activities can be found on **www.cjfallon.ie**.

CJFallon

Published by
CJ FALLON
Ground Floor - Block B, Liffey Valley Office Campus, Dublin 22, Ireland

ISBN 978-0-7144-1715-8

©

CJ Fallon

First Edition March 2010
This Reprint May 2017

Printed in Ireland by
Turner Print Group
Earl Street
Longford

Contents

Count in 10s

Day 1   Say the tables.

Learn these:

0 × 10 = 0	0 × 10 = 0		
1 × 10 = 10	1 x 10 = 10		
2 × 10 = 20	2 x 10 = 20		
3 × 10 = 30	3 x 10 = 30		
4 × 10 = 40	4 x 10 = 40		
5 × 10 = 50	5 × 10 = 50		
6 × 10 = 60	6 x 10 = 60		
7 × 10 = 70	7 x 10 = 70		
8 × 10 = 80	8 x 10 = 80		
9 × 10 = 90	9 x 10 = 90		
10 × 10 = 100	10 × 10 = 100		
11 × 10 = 110	11 x 10 = 110		
12 × 10 = 120	12 x 10 = 120		

1. (a) 0 × 10 = 0
   (b) 5 × 10 = 50
   (c) 10 × 10 = 100

2. (a) 5 times 10 = 50
   (b) 10 groups of 10 = 100
   (c) 0 times 10 = 0

3. How many sweets in…?
   (a) 5 bags ⇒ 5 × 10 = 50
   (b) 10 bags ⇒ 10 × 10 = 100
   (c) 0 bags ⇒ 0 × 10 = 0
   10 sweets

4. 10 × 10 = 100

5. (a) 0 × 10 = 0   (b) 5 × 10 = 50   (c) 10 × 10 = 100

12

Day 2   Say the tables.

Learn these:

0 × 10 = 0	
1 × 10 = 10	1 × 10 = 10
2 × 10 = 20	2 × 10 = 20
3 × 10 = 30	3 × 10 = 30
4 × 10 = 40	
5 × 10 = 50	
6 × 10 = 60	
7 × 10 = 70	
8 × 10 = 80	
9 × 10 = 90	
10 × 10 = 100	
11 × 10 = 110	
12 × 10 = 120	

1. (a) 1 × 10 = 10
   (b) 2 × 10 = 10 + 10 = ____
   (c) 3 × 10 = ___ + ___ + ___ = ___

2. How many straws in…?
   (a) 2 cups ⇒ ___ × 10 = ___
   (b) 3 cups ⇒ ___ × 10 = ___
   (c) 5 cups ⇒ ___ × 10 = ___
   (d) 10 cups ⇒ ___ × 10 = ___

3.
(a)	(b)	(c)	(d)	(e)
1	5	3	2	10
× 10	× 10	× 10	× 10	× 10

4. (a) ___ × 10 = ___
   (b) ___ × 10 = ___

14

2

Day 3 Say the tables.

Learn these:

$0 \times 10 = 0$
$1 \times 10 = 10$
$2 \times 10 = 20$
$3 \times 10 = 30$
$4 \times 10 = 40$ $4 \times 10 = 40$
$5 \times 10 = 50$
$6 \times 10 = 60$ $6 \times 10 = 60$
$7 \times 10 = 70$
$8 \times 10 = 80$
$9 \times 10 = 90$ $9 \times 10 = 90$
$10 \times 10 = 100$
$11 \times 10 = 110$ $11 \times 10 = 110$
$12 \times 10 = 120$

1. (a) [10] [10] [10] [10] [10✗]

$(5 \times 10) - (1 \times 10)$

⇒ ____ $\times 10 =$ ____

(b) [10] [10] [10] [10] [10] + [10]

$(5 \times 10) + (1 \times 10)$

⇒ ____ $\times 10 =$ ____

2. **Factor boxes**

(a) | 60 |
    | 6 | 10 |

(b) | 90 |
    | | 10 |

(c) | 50 |
    | | 10 |

3. (a) $(10 + 10 + 10 + 10)$

⇒ ____ $\times 10 =$ ____

(b) $(10 + 10 + 10 + 10 + 10 + 10)$

⇒ ____ $\times 10 =$ ____

4. (a) $9 \times 10 =$ ____

(b) $6 \times 10 =$ ____

(c) $4 \times 10 =$ ____

(d) $11 \times 10 =$ ____

| 10 |

Day 4 Say the tables.

Learn these:

$0 \times 10 = 0$
$1 \times 10 = 10$
$2 \times 10 = 20$
$3 \times 10 = 30$
$4 \times 10 = 40$
$5 \times 10 = 50$
$6 \times 10 = 60$
$7 \times 10 = 70$ $7 \times 10 = 70$
$8 \times 10 = 80$ $8 \times 10 = 80$
$9 \times 10 = 90$
$10 \times 10 = 100$
$11 \times 10 = 110$
$12 \times 10 = 120$ $12 \times 10 = 120$

1.

(a)	(b)	(c)	(d)	(e)
7	12	9	6	8
$\times 10$	$\times 10$	$\times 10$	$\times 10$	$\times 10$
____	____	____	____	____

2. **Write the missing numbers.**

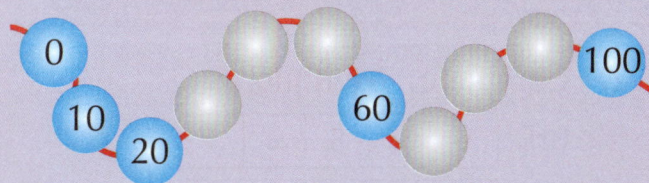

0, 10, 20, ... 60, ... 100

3. (a) 0, 10, ____, ____, 40, ____.

(b) 30, 40, ____, 60, ____, ____.

4. (a) $7 \times 10 =$ ____ $\times 7 =$ ____

(b) $9 \times 10 =$ ____ $\times 9 =$ ____

(c) $8 \times 10 = 10 \times$ ____ $=$ ____

5. (a) $7 \times 10 =$ ____

(b) $12 \times 10 =$ ____

(c) $8 \times 10 =$ ____

| 14 |

Do **Test 1** on page 58.

3

Count in 5s

$$\boxed{0}\ \boxed{5}\ \boxed{10}\ \boxed{15}\ \boxed{20}$$

Day 1 — Say the tables.

	Learn these:
$0 \times 5 = 0$	$0 \times 5 = 0$
$1 \times 5 = 5$	
$2 \times 5 = 10$	
$3 \times 5 = 15$	
$4 \times 5 = 20$	
$5 \times 5 = 25$	$5 \times 5 = 25$
$6 \times 5 = 30$	
$7 \times 5 = 35$	
$8 \times 5 = 40$	
$9 \times 5 = 45$	
$10 \times 5 = 50$	$10 \times 5 = 50$
$11 \times 5 = 55$	
$12 \times 5 = 60$	

1. (a) $= 3 \times \underline{\quad} = 15$

   (b) $= 5 \times \underline{\quad} = \underline{\quad}$

   (c) $= 0 \times \underline{\quad} = \underline{\quad}$

2. **Complete. (Multiply.)**

   (a) $5 \times 5 = \boxed{}$

   (b) $0 \times 5 \boxed{}$

   (c) $\boxed{} \times 5 \boxed{50}$

3. (a) $0 \times 5 = \underline{\quad}$

   (b) $5 \times 5 = \underline{\quad}$

   (c) $10 \times 5 = \underline{\quad}$

4.

(a)	(b)	(c)	(d)
0	5	10	5
$\times 5$	$\times 5$	$\times 5$	$\times 0$
—	—	—	—

13

Day 2 — Say the tables.

	Learn these:
$0 \times 5 = 0$	
$1 \times 5 = 5$	$1 \times 5 = 5$
$2 \times 5 = 10$	$2 \times 5 = 10$
$3 \times 5 = 15$	$3 \times 5 = 15$
$4 \times 5 = 20$	
$5 \times 5 = 25$	
$6 \times 5 = 30$	
$7 \times 5 = 35$	
$8 \times 5 = 40$	
$9 \times 5 = 45$	
$10 \times 5 = 50$	
$11 \times 5 = 55$	
$12 \times 5 = 60$	

1. **Factor boxes**

   (a) $\boxed{15}$ $\boxed{3}\ \square$ (b) $\boxed{50}$ $\boxed{5}\ \square$ (c) $\boxed{10}$ $\square\ \boxed{5}$

   (d) $\boxed{5}$ $\boxed{1}\ \square$ (e) $\boxed{0}$ $\boxed{5}\ \square$ (f) $\boxed{25}$ $\boxed{5}\ \square$

2.

(a)	(b)	(c)	(d)
2	3	1	5
$\times 5$	$\times 5$	$\times 5$	$\times 5$
—	—	—	—

3.

   (a) $\square$
   2×5

   (b) $\square$
   5×3

   (c) $\square$
   1×5

4. (a) $1 \times 5 = \underline{\quad}$

   (b) $2 \times 5 = \underline{\quad}$

   (c) $3 \times 5 = \underline{\quad}$

   (d) $(\underline{\quad} \times 5) + 4 = 19$

17

Day 3 — Say the tables.

				Learn these:
0	× 5	=	0	
1	× 5	=	5	
2	× 5	=	10	
3	× 5	=	15	
4	× 5	=	20	4 × 5 = 20
5	× 5	=	25	
6	× 5	=	30	6 × 5 = 30
7	× 5	=	35	
8	× 5	=	40	
9	× 5	=	45	9 × 5 = 45
10	× 5	=	50	
11	× 5	=	55	11 × 5 = 55
12	× 5	=	60	

1. (a) $(4 \times 5) + 2 = $ ____

   (b) $(6 \times 5) - 3 = $ ____

   (c) $(9 \times 5) + 3 = $ ____

2. Complete.

(a) 25 ← 5 — × 5 — 4 → (e)
(b) 55 — — 6 — — 45 (d)
(c) [ ]

3. Find the cost of…

(a) 1 bag ⇒ ____ × €5 = € ____

(b) 6 bags ⇒ ____ × €5 = € ____

(c) 9 bags ⇒ ____ × €5 = € ____

(d) 2 bags ⇒ ____ × €5 = € ____

(e) 10 bags ⇒ ____ × €5 = € ____

4. Complete. (Multiply.)

(a) | 5 | × | 5 | = | |

(b) | | × | 5 | | 30 |

14

Day 4 — Say the tables.

				Learn these:
0	× 5	=	0	
1	× 5	=	5	
2	× 5	=	10	
3	× 5	=	15	
4	× 5	=	20	
5	× 5	=	25	
6	× 5	=	30	
7	× 5	=	35	7 × 5 = 35
8	× 5	=	40	8 × 5 = 40
9	× 5	=	45	
10	× 5	=	50	
11	× 5	=	55	
12	× 5	=	60	12 × 5 = 60

1. (a) $7 \times 5 = $ ____   (d) $6 \times 5 = $ ____

   (b) $8 \times 5 = $ ____   (e) $9 \times 5 = $ ____

   (c) $12 \times 5 = $ ____   (f) $4 \times 5 = $ ____

2. Match.

× 5			× 5	
(a) 7•	•30	(f) 1•	•50
(b) 8•	•35	(g) 3•	•45
(c) 12•	•25	(h) 10•	•55
(d) 5•	•60	(i) 9•	•15
(e) 6•	•40	(j) 11•	• 5

3. Write the missing numbers.

55   40   30   10   0   5

4. > , < or =

(a) 4×5 ◯ 5×5

(b) 10×5 ◯ 5×10

(c) 12×5 ◯ 5×11

19

Do Test 2 on page 58.

5

Count in 2s

Day 1   Say the tables.

$0 \times 2 = 0$	**Learn these:**
$1 \times 2 = 2$	$0 \times 2 = 0$
$2 \times 2 = 4$	
$3 \times 2 = 6$	
$4 \times 2 = 8$	
$5 \times 2 = 10$	$5 \times 2 = 10$
$6 \times 2 = 12$	
$7 \times 2 = 14$	
$8 \times 2 = 16$	
$9 \times 2 = 18$	
$10 \times 2 = 20$	$10 \times 2 = 20$
$11 \times 2 = 22$	
$12 \times 2 = 24$	

1. (a) $(2 + 2 + 2 + 2 + 2) = $ _____ $\times 2 = $ _____

   (b) $5 + 5 = 2 \times 5 = $ _____

   (c) $5 \times 2 = $ _____ $\times 5 = $ _____

2. (a) $\begin{array}{r} 0 \\ \times 2 \\ \hline \end{array}$ (b) $\begin{array}{r} 5 \\ \times 2 \\ \hline \end{array}$ (c) $\begin{array}{r} 10 \\ \times 2 \\ \hline \end{array}$

3. (a) $= $ _____ $\times 2 = $ _____

   (b) $= $ _____ $\times 2 = $ _____

4. (a) $0 \times 2 = 2 \times 0 = $ _____

   (b) $10 \times 2 = $ _____ $\times 10 = $ _____

   (c) $5 \times 2 = $ _____ $\times 5 = $ _____

5. (a) 0 times 2 $= $ _____

   (b) 10 multiplied by 2 $= $ _____

   (c) 5 groups of 2 $= $ _____

14

Day 2   Say the tables.

$0 \times 2 = 0$	**Learn these:**
$1 \times 2 = 2$	$1 \times 2 = 2$
$2 \times 2 = 4$	$2 \times 2 = 4$
$3 \times 2 = 6$	$3 \times 2 = 6$
$4 \times 2 = 8$	
$5 \times 2 = 10$	
$6 \times 2 = 12$	
$7 \times 2 = 14$	
$8 \times 2 = 16$	
$9 \times 2 = 18$	
$10 \times 2 = 20$	
$11 \times 2 = 22$	
$12 \times 2 = 24$	

1. (a) $1 \times 2 = $ _____   (d) $0 \times 2 = $ _____

   (b) $2 \times 2 = $ _____   (e) $10 \times 2 = $ _____

   (c) $3 \times 2 = $ _____   (f) $5 \times 2 = $ _____

2. **Fill in the gaps.**

   (a) $\boxed{3} \times \bigcirc{2} \Rightarrow \boxed{6} + \bigcirc{5} = \boxed{}$

   (b) $\boxed{2} \times \bigcirc{2} \Rightarrow \boxed{} - \bigcirc{1} = \boxed{}$

   (c) $\boxed{5} \times \bigcirc{2} \Rightarrow \boxed{} - \bigcirc{3} = \boxed{}$

   (d) $\boxed{1} \times \bigcirc{2} \Rightarrow \boxed{} + \bigcirc{7} = \boxed{}$

3. **How many wheels are there on...?**

   2 wheels

   (a) 3 bicycles $\Rightarrow$ _____ $\times 2 = $ _____

   (b) 2 bicycles $\Rightarrow$ _____ $\times 2 = $ _____

   (c) 1 bicycles $\Rightarrow$ _____ $\times 2 = $ _____

4. (a) $\begin{array}{r} 2 \\ \times 2 \\ \hline \end{array}$ (b) $\begin{array}{r} 3 \\ \times 2 \\ \hline \end{array}$ (c) $\begin{array}{r} 1 \\ \times 2 \\ \hline \end{array}$ (d) $\begin{array}{r} 5 \\ \times 2 \\ \hline \end{array}$

17

Day 3   Say the tables.

Learn these:

0	×	2	=	0
1	×	2	=	2
2	×	2	=	4
3	×	2	=	6
4	×	2	=	8
5	×	2	=	10
6	×	2	=	12
7	×	2	=	14
8	×	2	=	16
9	×	2	=	18
10	×	2	=	20
11	×	2	=	22
12	×	2	=	24

Learn these:

$4 \times 2 = 8$

$6 \times 2 = 12$

$9 \times 2 = 18$

$11 \times 2 = 22$

1. $(2 + 2 + 2 + 2) =$ ____ $\times 2 =$ ____

2.

    $(10 \times 2) - (1 \times 2) =$ ____ $\times 2 =$ ____

3.
(a)	(b)	(c)	(d)	(e)
4	9	11	6	10
× 2	× 2	× 2	× 2	× 2
___	___	___	___	___

4. **How many eyes have…?**

    (a) 4 cats ⇒ ____ $\times 2 =$ ____

    (b) 6 cats ⇒ ____ $\times 2 =$ ____

    (c) 11 cats ⇒ ____ $\times 2 =$ ____

    (d) 9 cats ⇒ ____ $\times 2 =$ ____

    (e) 5 cats ⇒ ____ $\times 2 =$ ____

5. (a) $9 \times 2 =$ ____

    (b) $11 \times 2 =$ ____

    (c) $6 \times 2 =$ ____

15

Day 4   Say the tables.

Learn these:

0	×	2	=	0
1	×	2	=	2
2	×	2	=	4
3	×	2	=	6
4	×	2	=	8
5	×	2	=	10
6	×	2	=	12
7	×	2	=	14
8	×	2	=	16
9	×	2	=	18
10	×	2	=	20
11	×	2	=	22
12	×	2	=	24

Learn these:

$7 \times 2 = 14$

$8 \times 2 = 16$

$12 \times 2 = 24$

1. (a) $7 \times 2 =$ ____   (d) $4 \times 2 =$ ____

    (b) $8 \times 2 =$ ____   (e) $6 \times 2 =$ ____

    (c) $12 \times 2 =$ ____   (f) $9 \times 2 =$ ____

2. (a) 2, 4, 6, ____, 10, ____, 14, ____.

    (b) 0, 2, 4, ____, 8, ____, 12, ____.

3.
(a)	(b)	(c)	(d)	(e)
12	7	8	9	5
× 2	× 2	× 2	× 2	× 2
___	___	___	___	___

4. **Fill in the gaps.**

    (a) 8 × 2 16 − 5 ☐

    (b) 12 × 2 ☐ + 3 ☐

    (c) 7 × 2 ☐ + 4 ☐

    (d) 9 × 2 ☐ − 7 ☐

    (e) 4 × 2 ☐ + 6 ☐

18

Do **Test 3** on page 59.

7

Count in 4s

0 4 8 12 16

Day 1 Say the tables.

0	×	4	=	0
1	×	4	=	4
2	×	4	=	8
3	×	4	=	12
4	×	4	=	16
5	×	4	=	20
6	×	4	=	24
7	×	4	=	28
8	×	4	=	32
9	×	4	=	36
10	×	4	=	40
11	×	4	=	44
12	×	4	=	48

Learn these:

$0 \times 4 = 0$

$5 \times 4 = 20$

$10 \times 4 = 40$

1. How many **legs** have...?

(a) 5 dogs ⇒ ___ × 4 = ___

(b) 10 dogs ⇒ ___ × 4 = ___

(c) 0 dogs ⇒ ___ × 4 = ___

2. (a) $0 \times 4 =$ ___

(b) $5 \times 4 =$ ___

(c) $10 \times 4 =$ ___

3. Factor boxes

(a) 40 / 4   (b) 0 / 4   (c) 20 / 5

4. Complete (**Multiply**.).

(a) 5 × 4 =

(b) 10 × ___ = 40

(c) ___ × 4 = 0

5. (a) 0 multiplied by 4 = ___

(b) 10 times 4 = ___

(c) 5 groups of 4 = ___   15

Day 2 Say the tables.

0	×	4	=	0
1	×	4	=	4
2	×	4	=	8
3	×	4	=	12
4	×	4	=	16
5	×	4	=	20
6	×	4	=	24
7	×	4	=	28
8	×	4	=	32
9	×	4	=	36
10	×	4	=	40
11	×	4	=	44
12	×	4	=	48

Learn these:

$1 \times 4 = 4$

$2 \times 4 = 8$

$3 \times 4 = 12$

1. How many **holes**?

(b) = ___ × 4 = ___

(b) = ___ × 4 = ___

(c) = ___ × 4 = ___

2. (a) $(4 + 4) =$ ___ × 4 = ___

(b) $(4 + 4 + 4) =$ ___ × 4 = ___

(c) $4 =$ ___ × 4 = ___

3.

(a)	(b)	(c)	(d)	(e)
1	5	3	2	0
× 4	× 4	× 4	× 4	× 4

4. (a) $3 \times 4 =$ ___ × 3 = ___

(b) $2 \times 4 = 4 \times$ ___ = ___

(c) $1 \times 4 = 4 \times$ ___ = ___

(d) $(3 \times 4) + 6 =$ ___

(e) $(2 \times 4) - 6 =$ ___   16

Day 3   Say the tables.

Learn these:

0 × 4 = 0	
1 × 4 = 4	
2 × 4 = 8	
3 × 4 = 12	
4 × 4 = 16	4 × 4 = 16
5 × 4 = 20	
6 × 4 = 24	6 × 4 = 24
7 × 4 = 28	
8 × 4 = 32	
9 × 4 = 36	9 × 4 = 36
10 × 4 = 40	
11 × 4 = 44	11 × 4 = 44
12 × 4 = 48	

1. (a)   4 × 4 = ____   (d)   9 × 4 = ____

(b)   6 × 4 = ____   (e)   11 × 4 = ____

(c)   10 × 4 = ____   (f)   3 × 4 = ____

2. **How many wheels are there on…?**

4 wheels

(a)   4 cars ⇒ ____ × 4 = ____

(b) 11 cars ⇒ ____ × 4 = ____

(c)   9 cars ⇒ ____ × 4 = ____

(d)   6 cars ⇒ ____ × 4 = ____

3. (a)

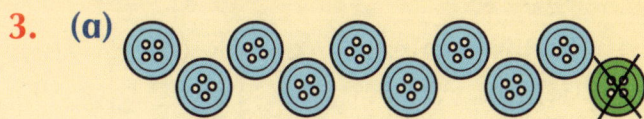

(10 × 4) – (1 × 4) ⇒ ____ × 4 = ____

(b)

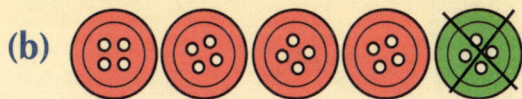

(5 × 4) – (1 × 4) ⇒ ____ × 4 = ____

4.

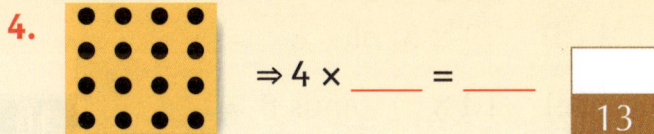   ⇒ 4 × ____ = ____

13

Day 4   Say the tables.

Learn these:

0 × 4 = 0	
1 × 4 = 4	
2 × 4 = 8	
3 × 4 = 12	
4 × 4 = 16	
5 × 4 = 20	
6 × 4 = 24	
7 × 4 = 28	7 × 4 = 28
8 × 4 = 32	8 × 4 = 32
9 × 4 = 36	
10 × 4 = 40	
11 × 4 = 44	
12 × 4 = 48	12 × 4 = 48

1. **Match.**

× 4	
(a) 8•	•28
(b) 12•	•32
(c) 7•	•48

× 4	
(d) 9•	•16
(e) 6•	•24
(f) 4•	•36

2.

(a)	(b)	(c)	(d)	(e)
7	9	8	6	10
× 4	× 4	× 4	× 4	× 4
___	___	___	___	___

3. **Factor boxes**

(a)
24	
	4

(b)
32	
	4

(c)
48	
	4

(d)
36	
	4

(e)
20	
	4

(f)
28	
	7

4. (a) ____ × 4 = 20

(b) ____ × 4 = 48

(c) ____ × 4 = 28

(d)   8 × 4 = ____

21

Do **Test 4** on page **59.**

9

Count in 8s

Day 1   Say the tables.

	Learn these:
$0 \times 8 = 0$	$0 \times 8 = 0$
$1 \times 8 = 8$	
$2 \times 8 = 16$	
$3 \times 8 = 24$	
$4 \times 8 = 32$	
$5 \times 8 = 40$	$5 \times 8 = 40$
$6 \times 8 = 48$	
$7 \times 8 = 56$	
$8 \times 8 = 64$	
$9 \times 8 = 72$	
$10 \times 8 = 80$	$10 \times 8 = 80$
$11 \times 8 = 88$	
$12 \times 8 = 96$	

1. (a) $0 \times 8 =$ ____

   (b) $5 \times 8 =$ ____

   (c) $10 \times 8 =$ ____

   (d)
   $$\begin{array}{r} 0 \\ \times\ 8 \\ \hline \end{array}$$

   (e)
   $$\begin{array}{r} 5 \\ \times\ 8 \\ \hline \end{array}$$

2. **How many legs have…?**

   (a) 10 spiders

   ⇒ ____ $\times 8 =$ ____

   (b) 5 spiders

   ⇒ ____ $\times 8 =$ ____

   (c) 0 spiders

   ⇒ ____ $\times 8 =$ ____

   spider with 8 legs

3. (a)

   0

   ____ $\times 8$

   (b)

   ☐

   5×8

   (c)

   ☐

   8×10

4. (a) 0 times 8   = ____

   (b) 10 groups of 8 = ____

   (c) 5 sets of 8   = ____

   (d) (____ $\times 8$) + 6 = 86

15

Day 2   Say the tables.

	Learn these:
$0 \times 8 = 0$	
$1 \times 8 = 8$	$1 \times 8 = 8$
$2 \times 8 = 16$	$2 \times 8 = 16$
$3 \times 8 = 24$	$3 \times 8 = 24$
$4 \times 8 = 32$	
$5 \times 8 = 40$	
$6 \times 8 = 48$	
$7 \times 8 = 56$	
$8 \times 8 = 64$	
$9 \times 8 = 72$	
$10 \times 8 = 80$	
$11 \times 8 = 88$	
$12 \times 8 = 96$	

1. (a) ⇒ ____ $\times 8 =$ ____

   (b) ⇒ ____ $\times 8 =$ ____

   (c) ⇒ ____ $\times 8 =$ ____

2. (a) $(8 + 8 + 8)$ ⇒ ____ $\times 8 =$ ____

   (b) $(8 + 8)$ ⇒ ____ $\times 8 =$ ____

   (c) 8 ⇒ ____ $\times 8 =$ ____

3.
(a)	(b)	(c)	(d)	(e)
0	10	3	2	5
$\times 8$	$\times 8$	$\times 8$	$\times 8$	$\times 8$
___	___	___	___	___

4. (a) (1×8) plus 4   = ____

   (b) (2×8) minus 6 = ____

   (c) (5×8) less 7   = ____

   (d) (3×8) plus 6   = ____

   (e) (10×8) minus 8 = ____

16

Day 3   Say the tables.

Learn these:

0	× 8	=	0
1	× 8	=	8
2	× 8	=	16
3	× 8	=	24
4	× 8	=	32
5	× 8	=	40
6	× 8	=	48
7	× 8	=	56
8	× 8	=	64
9	× 8	=	72
10	× 8	=	80
11	× 8	=	88
12	× 8	=	96

Learn these:

$4 \times 8 = 32$

$6 \times 8 = 48$

$9 \times 8 = 72$

$11 \times 8 = 88$

1. (a) $(8 + 8 + 8 + 8) \Rightarrow$ ____ $\times 8 =$ ____

   (b) $(8 + 8 + 8 + 8 + 8 + 8)$

      $\Rightarrow$ ____ $\times 8 =$ ____

2. (a) $(4 \times 8) + (1 \times 8)$

      $\Rightarrow$ 32 (+) ____ = ____

   (b) $(9 \times 8) - (3 \times 8)$

      $\Rightarrow$ ____ ◯ ____ = ____

3. How many markers in...?

   (a) 11 packs ⇒ ____ × 4 = ____

   (b) 9 packs ⇒ ____ × 4 = ____

   (c) 4 packs ⇒ ____ × 4 = ____

   4 markers

   (d) 6 packs ⇒ ____ × 4 = ____

4. Complete. (Multiply.)

   (a) | 6 | × | 8 | = | |

   (b) | | × | 8 | = | 32 |

   (c) | 9 | × | | = | 72 |

   (d) | | | 8 | = | 24 |

12

Day 4   Say the tables.

Learn these:

0	× 8	=	0
1	× 8	=	8
2	× 8	=	16
3	× 8	=	24
4	× 8	=	32
5	× 8	=	40
6	× 8	=	48
7	× 8	=	56
8	× 8	=	64
9	× 8	=	72
10	× 8	=	80
11	× 8	=	88
12	× 8	=	96

Learn these:

$7 \times 8 = 56$

$8 \times 8 = 64$

$12 \times 8 = 96$

1. (a) $7 \times 8 =$ ____   (c) $12 \times 8 =$ ____

   (b) $8 \times 8 =$ ____   (d) $8 \times 0 =$ ____

2. How many arms have...?

   octopus with 8 arms

   (a) 7 octopuses ⇒ ____ × 8 = ____

   (b) 8 octopuses ⇒ ____ × 8 = ____

   (c) 12 octopuses ⇒ ____ × 8 = ____

3.

(a)	(b)	(c)	(d)	(e)
7	9	8	6	12
× 8	× 8	× 8	× 8	× 8

4. (a) $(8 + 8 + 8 + 8 + 8 + 8 + 8)$

      $\Rightarrow$ ____ $\times 8 =$ ____

   (b) $(8 + 8 + 8 + 8 + 8 + 8 + 8 + 8)$

      $\Rightarrow$ ____ $\times 8 =$ ____

14

Do Test 5 on page 60.

11

Revision A Multiplication by 10, 5, 2, 4 and 8

Revision 1

1.

(a)	(b)	(c)	(d)	(e)
7	8	6	8	9
× 10	× 5	× 5	× 10	× 5

2. Complete.

(b) ☐ (c) 55 (d) 25

12

(a) ☐ ← 6 — **× 5** — 8 → ☐ (e)

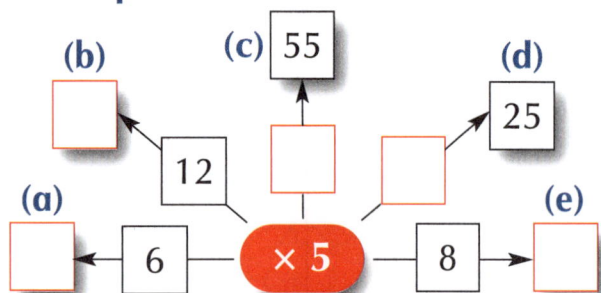

3. How many roses in…?

bunch of 10 roses

(a) 1 bunch = ____
(b) 4 bunches = ____
(c) 11 bunches = ____
(d) 0 bunches = ____
(e) 8 bunches = ____

4. > , < or =

(a) 5 × 5 ◯ 25
(b) 5 × 10 ◯ 60
(c) 9 × 5 ◯ 40
(d) 6 × 10 ◯ (10 + 10 + 10 + 10)
(e) 35 ◯ 10 × 5

5.
(a) (7 × 5) + 6 = ____
(b) (8 × 10) − 4 = ____
(c) (6 × 5) − 3 = ____
(d) (11 × 5) + 5 = ____
(e) (9 × 10) − 7 = ____

25

Revision 2

1. Complete. (Multiply.)

(a) 5 × 2 = ☐
(b) 7 × ☐ 14
(c) ☐ 2 16
(d) 9 ☐ 2 ☐

2.

(a)	(b)	(c)	(d)	(e)
4	10	6	9	2
× 2	× 2	× 2	× 2	× 2

3. Factor boxes

(a) ☐ 2 / 8   (b) ☐ 2 / 16   (c) 0 2 / ☐

(d) 10 2 / ☐   (e) 9 ☐ / 18   (f) 2 11 / ☐

4. How many legs have…?

(a) 3 girls = ____ legs
(b) 7 girls = ____ legs
(c) 6 girls = ____ legs
(d) 0 girls = ____ legs
(e) 9 girls = ____ legs

5. Match.

× 2	
(a) 6•	•14
(b) 3•	•18
(c) 7•	•12
(d) 2•	• 6
(e) 9•	• 4

25

Revision 3

1. Complete.

(a) ☐ ← 6 ← (× 4) → 5 → ☐ (e)

(b) 16 ← ☐

(c) ☐ ← 9

(d) ☐ → 32

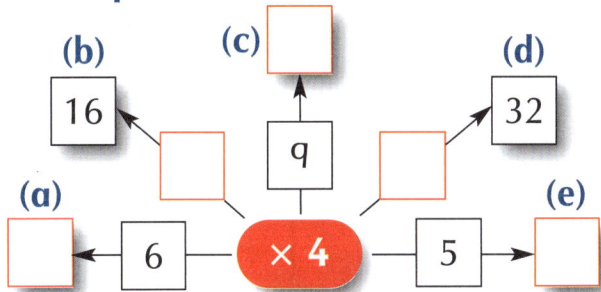

2. Complete. (Multiply.)

(a)	12	×	4	= ☐
(b)	☐	×	4	= 20
(c)	4			16
(d)	☐	4		28
(e)	10	4		☐

3. How many legs on...?

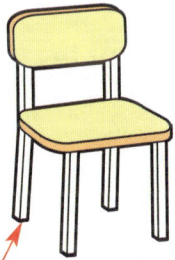

chair with 4 legs

(a) 3 chairs = ____

(b) 10 chairs = ____

(c) 7 chairs = ____

(d) 9 chairs = ____

(e) 1 chair = ____

4.

(a)	(b)	(c)	(d)	(e)
3	2	6	9	5
× 4	× 4	× 4	× 4	× 4
__	__	__	__	__

5. $>$, $<$ or $=$

(a) 4×5 ◯ 5×4

(b) 3×4 ◯ $(4 + 4 + 4 + 4)$

(c) 6×4 ◯ $(5 \times 4) + 5$

(d) 8×4 ◯ $(9 \times 4) - 4$

(e) 10×4 ◯ $(6 \times 6) + 3$

25

Revision 4

1.

(a)	(b)	(c)	(d)	(e)
5	0	7	1	9
× 8	× 8	× 8	× 8	× 8
__	__	__	__	__

2. Fill in the gaps.

(a) $4 \times \text{⑧} \Rightarrow \square - \text{③} = \square$

(b) $7 \times \text{⑧} \Rightarrow \square + \text{④} = \square$

(c) $6 \times \text{⑧} \Rightarrow \square - \text{⑥} = \square$

(d) $3 \times \text{⑧} \Rightarrow \square + \text{⑤} = \square$

(e) $9 \times \text{⑧} \Rightarrow \square - \text{②} = \square$

3. How many peas in...?

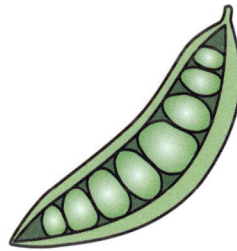

8 peas in a pod

(a) 1 pod = ____

(b) 4 pods = ____

(c) 11 pods = ____

(d) 0 pods = ____

(e) 8 pods = ____

4.

(a) $7 \times 8 =$ ____

(b) $9 \times 8 =$ ____

(c) $8 \times 8 =$ ____

(d) $5 \times 8 =$ ____

(e) $6 \times 8 =$ ____

(f) $11 \times 8 =$ ____

5. Match.

	× 8	
(a)	2 •	• 72
(b)	6 •	• 56
(c)	9 •	• 16
(d)	7 •	• 48

25

Record your scores on page 77.

Count in 3s

Day 1   Say the tables.

$0 \times 3 = 0$	
$1 \times 3 = 3$	
$2 \times 3 = 6$	
$3 \times 3 = 9$	
$4 \times 3 = 12$	
$5 \times 3 = 15$	
$6 \times 3 = 18$	
$7 \times 3 = 21$	
$8 \times 3 = 24$	
$9 \times 3 = 27$	
$10 \times 3 = 30$	
$11 \times 3 = 33$	
$12 \times 3 = 36$	

Learn these:

$0 \times 3 = 0$

$5 \times 3 = 15$

$10 \times 3 = 30$

1. (a) $0 \times 3 = $ ____

   (b) $5 \times 3 = $ ____

   (c) $10 \times 3 = $ ____

   (d)   0
       $\times\, 3$
       ____

   (e)   5
       $\times\, 3$
       ____

2. (a) $(3 + 3 + 3 + 3 + 3)$

   $\Rightarrow$ ____ $\times\, 3 = $ ____

   (b) $\Rightarrow$ ____ $\times\, 3 = $ ____

3. (a) $5 \times 3 = $ ____ $\times\, 5 = $ ____

   (b) $10 \times 3 = $ ____ $\times\, 10 = $ ____

4. **Factor boxes**

   (a) | 30 |
       |----|
       | 10 | |

   (b) | | |
       |--|--|
       | | 3 |

   (c) | 15 | |
       |----|--|
       | 3 | |

5. (a) (____ $\times\, 3$) $+ 4 = 4$

   (b) (____ $\times\, 3$) $+ 2 = 17$

   (c) (____ $\times\, 3$) $- 1 = 29$

   (d) ($5 \times$ ____) $+ 6 = 21$

16

Day 2   Say the tables.

$0 \times 3 = 0$	
$1 \times 3 = 3$	
$2 \times 3 = 6$	
$3 \times 3 = 9$	
$4 \times 3 = 12$	
$5 \times 3 = 15$	
$6 \times 3 = 18$	
$7 \times 3 = 21$	
$8 \times 3 = 24$	
$9 \times 3 = 27$	
$10 \times 3 = 30$	
$11 \times 3 = 33$	
$12 \times 3 = 36$	

Learn these:

$1 \times 3 = 3$

$2 \times 3 = 6$

$3 \times 3 = 9$

1. **How many wheels on…?**

   3 wheels

   (a) 1 tricycle = ____

   (b) 2 tricycles = ____

   (c) 3 tricycles = ____

2. (a) $1 \times 3 = $ ____

   (b) $2 \times 3 = $ ____

   (c) $3 \times 3 = $ ____

   (d) $5 \times 3 = $ ____

   (e) $10 \times 3 = $ ____

   (f) $0 \times 3 = $ ____

3. (a) $(3 + 3)$ $\Rightarrow$ ____ $\times\, 3 = $ ____

   (b) $(3 + 3 + 3)$ $\Rightarrow$ ____ $\times\, 3 = $ ____

   (c) 3 $\Rightarrow$ ____ $\times\, 3 = $ ____

4.
(a)	(b)	(c)	(d)	(e)
1	2	3	5	10
$\times\, 3$	$\times\, 3$	$\times\, 3$	$\times\, 3$	$\times\, 3$
____	____	____	____	____

5. (a) $2 \times 3 = $ ____

   (b) $3 \times 3 = $ ____

19

14

Day 3   Say the tables.

Learn these:

0	×	3	=	0
1	×	3	=	3
2	×	3	=	6
3	×	3	=	9
4	×	3	=	12
5	×	3	=	15
6	×	3	=	18
7	×	3	=	21
8	×	3	=	24
9	×	3	=	27
10	×	3	=	30
11	×	3	=	33
12	×	3	=	36

Learn these:

4 × 3 = 12

6 × 3 = 18

9 × 3 = 27

11 × 3 = 33

1. (a) 9 × 3 = _____   (c) 11 × 3 = _____

   (b) 6 × 3 = _____   (d) 4 × 3 = _____

2. (a)   _____ × 3 = _____

   (b)   _____ × 3 = _____

   (c)   _____ × 3 = _____

   (d)   _____ × 3 = _____

3. (a) 4 × 3 = _____ × 4 = _____

   (b) 11 × 3 = 3 × _____ = _____

   (c) 9 × 3 = 3 × _____ = _____

   (d) 6 × 3 = _____ × 6 = _____

4. (a) 0, 3, _____, _____, 12, _____, 18.

   (b) 21, 24, _____, _____, 33.

   (c) 3, 6, _____, _____, 15, _____.

15

Day 4   Say the tables.

Learn these:

0	×	3	=	0
1	×	3	=	3
2	×	3	=	6
3	×	3	=	9
4	×	3	=	12
5	×	3	=	15
6	×	3	=	18
7	×	3	=	21
8	×	3	=	24
9	×	3	=	27
10	×	3	=	30
11	×	3	=	33
12	×	3	=	36

Learn these:

7 × 3 = 21

8 × 3 = 24

12 × 3 = 36

1. Factor boxes

   (a) 12 / 3 ___   (b) ___ / 5 3   (c) 18 / 6 ___

   (d) ___ / 8 3   (e) 27 / 3 ___   (f) 30 / 3 ___

2. (a) 7 × 3 = _____   (d) 6 × 3 = _____

   (b) 12 × 3 = _____   (e) 9 × 3 = _____

   (c) 8 × 3 = _____   (f) 4 × 3 = _____

3.

(a)	(b)	(c)	(d)	(e)
7	8	6	9	12
× 3	× 3	× 3	× 3	× 3
___	___	___	___	___

4. Write the missing numbers.

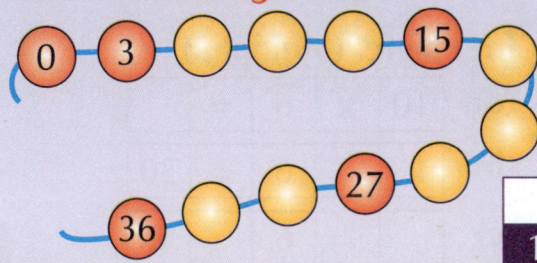

0 3 __ __ __ 15 __
__ __ 27 __
36 __

18

Do Test 6 on page 60.

15

Count in 6s

$$0 \quad 6 \quad 12 \quad 18 \quad 24$$

Day 1 — Say the tables.

	Learn these:
$0 \times 6 = 0$	$0 \times 6 = 0$
$1 \times 6 = 6$	
$2 \times 6 = 12$	
$3 \times 6 = 18$	
$4 \times 6 = 24$	
$5 \times 6 = 30$	$5 \times 6 = 30$
$6 \times 6 = 36$	
$7 \times 6 = 42$	
$8 \times 6 = 48$	
$9 \times 6 = 54$	
$10 \times 6 = 60$	$10 \times 6 = 60$
$11 \times 6 = 66$	
$12 \times 6 = 72$	

1. $(6 + 6 + 6 + 6 + 6)$

   $= \underline{\quad} \times 6 = \underline{\quad}$

2. **Fill in the gaps.**

   (a) $\boxed{5} \times \bigcirc{6} \Rightarrow \square + \bigcirc{7} = \square$

   (b) $\boxed{0} \times \bigcirc{6} \Rightarrow \square + \bigcirc{6} = \square$

   (c) $\boxed{10} \times \bigcirc{6} \Rightarrow \square - \bigcirc{3} = \square$

3. **Find the cost of…**

   €6

   (a) 5 T-shirts = €____

   (b) 10 T-shirts = €____

   (c) 0 T-shirts = €____

4. (a) $0 \times 6 = 6 \times \underline{\quad} = \underline{\quad}$

   (b) $5 \times 6 = 6 \times \underline{\quad} = \underline{\quad}$

5. **Complete. (Multiply.)**

   (a) | 10 | × | 6 | = | |
   |---|---|---|---|---|

   (b) | | | 6 | = | 30 |
   |---|---|---|---|---|

   (c) | | | 6 | | 0 |
   |---|---|---|---|---|

   12

Day 2 — Say the tables.

	Learn these:
$0 \times 6 = 0$	
$1 \times 6 = 6$	$1 \times 6 = 6$
$2 \times 6 = 12$	$2 \times 6 = 12$
$3 \times 6 = 18$	$3 \times 6 = 18$
$4 \times 6 = 24$	
$5 \times 6 = 30$	
$6 \times 6 = 36$	
$7 \times 6 = 42$	
$8 \times 6 = 48$	
$9 \times 6 = 54$	
$10 \times 6 = 60$	
$11 \times 6 = 66$	
$12 \times 6 = 72$	

1. **Factor boxes**

   (a) | 3 | |
   |---|---|
   | 18 | |

   (b) | 6 | |
   |---|---|
   | 12 | |

   (c) | 1 | |
   |---|---|
   | 6 | |

2. (a) $\square$ ⟋⟍ 3×6

   (b) 12 ⟋⟍ $6 \times \square$

   (c) $\square$ ⟋⟍ 1×6

3. **Complete.**

   (a) $\square \leftarrow \boxed{1} \leftarrow \boxed{\times 6} \rightarrow \boxed{3} \rightarrow \square$ (e)

   (b) $\square \leftarrow \boxed{5}$

   (c) $\boxed{12} \uparrow \square$

   (d) $\rightarrow \boxed{60}$

4.
(a)	(b)	(c)	(d)
1	3	5	2
× 6	× 6	× 6	× 6
____	____	____	____

   15

Day 3 — Say the tables.

Learn these:

0 × 6 = 0
1 × 6 = 6
2 × 6 = 12
3 × 6 = 18
4 × 6 = 24   4 × 6 = 24
5 × 6 = 30
6 × 6 = 36   6 × 6 = 36
7 × 6 = 42
8 × 6 = 48
9 × 6 = 54   9 × 6 = 54
10 × 6 = 60
11 × 6 = 66   11 × 6 = 66
12 × 6 = 72

1. (a) 9 × 6 = ____   (d) 6 × 6 = ____
   (b) 11 × 6 = ____   (e) 3 × 6 = ____
   (c) 4 × 6 = ____   (f) 10 × 6 = ____

2. (a) 4   (b) 6   (c) 6   (d) 6   (e) 3
      × 6   × 9   × 11   × 4   × 6

3. Write the missing numbers.

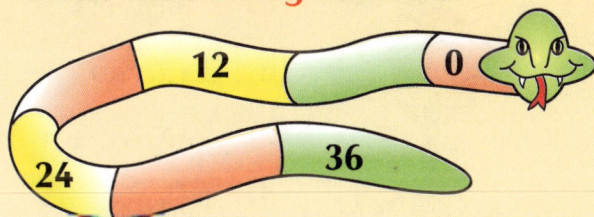

   12   0
   24   36

4. Fill in the gaps.
   (a) 6 × 6 36 + 5 ___
   (b) 4 × 6 ___ − 3 ___
   (c) 11 × 6 ___ + 4 ___
   (d) 9 × 6 ___ − 8 ___

   16

Day 4 — Say the tables.

Learn these:

0 × 6 = 0
1 × 6 = 6
2 × 6 = 12
3 × 6 = 18
4 × 6 = 24
5 × 6 = 30
6 × 6 = 36
7 × 6 = 42   7 × 6 = 42
8 × 6 = 48   8 × 6 = 48
9 × 6 = 54
10 × 6 = 60
11 × 6 = 66
12 × 6 = 72   12 × 6 = 72

1. Match.

× 6			× 6	
(a) 5•	•42	(e) 0•	•24
(b) 7•	•72	(f) 4•	•54
(c) 12•	•48	(g) 11•	• 0
(d) 8•	•30	(h) 9•	•66

2. >, < or =
   (a) 7 × 6 ◯ 6 × 8
   (b) 12 × 6 ◯ 11 × 6
   (c) 9 × 6 ◯ 6 × 9
   (d) 8 × 6 ◯ 6 × 5

3. (a) ____ × 6 = 72
   (b) ____ × 6 = 42
   (c) ____ × 6 = 66
   (d) ____ × 6 = 48
   (e) ____ × 6 = 18
   (f) ____ × 6 = 54

   18

Do **Test 7** on page **61**.

17

Count in 9s

Day 1   Say the tables.

Learn these:

$0 \times 9 =$	0	
$1 \times 9 =$	9	
$2 \times 9 =$	18	
$3 \times 9 =$	27	
$4 \times 9 =$	36	
$5 \times 9 =$	45	
$6 \times 9 =$	54	
$7 \times 9 =$	63	
$8 \times 9 =$	72	
$9 \times 9 =$	81	
$10 \times 9 =$	90	
$11 \times 9 =$	99	
$12 \times 9 =$	108	

Learn these (handwritten):
$0 \times 9 = 0$
$1 \times 9 = 9$
$2 \times 9 = 18$
$3 \times 9 = 27$
$4 \times 9 = 36$
$5 \times 9 = 45$
$6 \times 9 = 54$
$7 \times 9 = 63$
$8 \times 9 = 72$
$9 \times 9 = 81$
$10 \times 9 = 90$
$11 \times 9 = 99$
$12 \times 9 = 108$

1. (a) $0 \times 9 =$ ____
   (b) $10 \times 9 =$ ____
   (c) $5 \times 9 =$ ____

   (d) $\begin{array}{r} 10 \\ \times 9 \\ \hline \end{array}$ (e) $\begin{array}{r} 5 \\ \times 9 \\ \hline \end{array}$

2. **Find the cost of...**

   €9

   (a) 10 books = €____
   (b) 5 books = €____
   (c) 0 books = €____

3. (a) $0 \times 9 = 9 \times$ ____ $=$ ____
   (b) $5 \times 9 = 9 \times$ ____ $=$ ____
   (c) $10 \times 9 =$ ____

4. **Complete. (Multiply.)**

   (a) | 10 | × | 9 | = | |
   (b) | | × | 9 | = | 0 |
   (c) | 5 | | | | 45 |

   14

Day 2   Say the tables.

Learn these:

$0 \times 9 =$	0	
$1 \times 9 =$	9	
$2 \times 9 =$	18	
$3 \times 9 =$	27	
$4 \times 9 =$	36	
$5 \times 9 =$	45	
$6 \times 9 =$	54	
$7 \times 9 =$	63	
$8 \times 9 =$	72	
$9 \times 9 =$	81	
$10 \times 9 =$	90	
$11 \times 9 =$	99	
$12 \times 9 =$	108	

Learn these:
$1 \times 9 = 9$
$2 \times 9 = 18$
$3 \times 9 = 27$

1. (a) $(9 + 9 + 9) \Rightarrow$ ____ $\times 9 =$ ____
   (b) $(9 + 9)$ $\Rightarrow$ ____ $\times 9 =$ ____
   (c) 9 $\Rightarrow$ ____ $\times 9 =$ ____

2. (a) $3 \times 9 =$ ____
   (b) $1 \times 9 =$ ____
   (c) $2 \times 9 =$ ____

   (d) $\begin{array}{r} 2 \\ \times 9 \\ \hline \end{array}$ (e) $\begin{array}{r} 3 \\ \times 9 \\ \hline \end{array}$

3. **How many petals on...?**

   (a) 2 flowers = ____
   (b) 3 flowers = ____
   (c) 5 flowers = ____
   (d) 1 flower = ____

   flower with 9 petals

4. (a) 
   $\Rightarrow$ ____ $\times 9 =$ ____

   (b) 
   $\Rightarrow$ ____ $\times 9 =$ ____

   14

Day 3   Say the tables.

$0 \times 9 = 0$
$1 \times 9 = 9$
$2 \times 9 = 18$
$3 \times 9 = 27$
$4 \times 9 = 36$
$5 \times 9 = 45$
$6 \times 9 = 54$
$7 \times 9 = 63$
$8 \times 9 = 72$
$9 \times 9 = 81$
$10 \times 9 = 90$
$11 \times 9 = 99$
$12 \times 9 = 108$

Learn these:

$4 \times 9 = 36$

$6 \times 9 = 54$

$9 \times 9 = 81$

$11 \times 9 = 99$

1. **How many spots have…?**

(a) 6 ladybirds = ____

(b) 11 ladybirds = ____

(c) 9 ladybirds = ____

ladybird with 9 dots

(d) 4 ladybirds = ____

(e) 10 ladybirds = ____

2. (a) 9 9 9 9 9 9 9 9 9 9 + 9

$\Rightarrow (10 \times 9) + (1 \times 9)$

$\Rightarrow$ ____ ◯ ____ = ____

(b) 9 9 9 9 9 9 9 9 9 ~~9~~

$\Rightarrow (10 \times 9) - (1 \times 9)$

$\Rightarrow$ ____ ◯ ____ = ____

3. (a) $4 \times 9 =$ ____

(b) $11 \times 9 =$ ____

(c) $9 \times 9 =$ ____

(d) $6 \times 9 =$ ____

(e) ____ $\times 9 = 90$

| 12 |

Day 4   Say the tables.

$0 \times 9 = 0$
$1 \times 9 = 9$
$2 \times 9 = 18$
$3 \times 9 = 27$
$4 \times 9 = 36$
$5 \times 9 = 45$
$6 \times 9 = 54$
$7 \times 9 = 63$
$8 \times 9 = 72$
$9 \times 9 = 81$
$10 \times 9 = 90$
$11 \times 9 = 99$
$12 \times 9 = 108$

Learn these:

$7 \times 9 = 63$

$8 \times 9 = 72$

$12 \times 9 = 108$

1. **Ring the correct answer.**

(a) $12 \times 9 =$	72	(108)	98
(b) $9 \times 3 =$	21	32	27
(c) $9 \times 7 =$	73	63	42
(d) $9 \times 10 =$	90	95	108
(e) $9 \times 8 =$	63	84	72

2. (a) $7 \times 9 =$ ____   (d) $12 \times 9 =$ ____

(b) $8 \times 9 =$ ____   (e) $6 \times 9 =$ ____

(c) $4 \times 9 =$ ____   (f) $9 \times 9 =$ ____

3. **Fill in the gaps.**

(a) ☐10 $\times$ ⑨ $\Rightarrow$ ☐ $+$ ⑥ $=$ ☐

(b) ☐5 $\times$ ⑨ $\Rightarrow$ ☐ $-$ ⑦ $=$ ☐

(c) ☐8 $\times$ ⑨ $\Rightarrow$ ☐ $+$ ⑧ $=$ ☐

(d) ☐7 $\times$ ⑨ $\Rightarrow$ ☐ $-$ ⑤ $=$ ☐

4. (a) $9 \times$ ____ $= 108$

(b) $11 \times$ ____ $= 99$

| 16 |

Do **Test 8** on page **61**.

Revision B — Multiplication by 3, 6 and 9

Revision 5

1.
(a) 3 × 3 = ____
(b) 0 × 3 = ____
(c) 1 × 2 = ____
(d) 5 × 3 = ____
(e) 7 × 3 = ____
(f) 9 × 3 = ____

2. Fill in the gaps.

(a) ⬜2 × ⭕3 ⇒ ⬜ + ⭕6 = ⬜

(b) ⬜6 × ⭕3 ⇒ ⬜ − ⭕5 = ⬜

(c) ⬜10 × ⭕3 ⇒ ⬜ − ⭕8 = ⬜

(d) ⬜8 × ⭕3 ⇒ ⬜ + ⭕9 = ⬜

(e) ⬜0 × ⭕3 ⇒ ⬜ + ⭕7 = ⬜

3. Find the cost of…

Breakfast CEREAL €3

(a) 3 boxes = € ____
(b) 5 boxes = € ____
(c) 9 boxes = € ____
(d) 7 boxes = € ____

4. Factor boxes

(a)
9	
18	

(b)
7	3

(c)
8	
	24

(d)
9	3

(e)
	3
30	

5. Complete. (Multiply.)

(a)
| 7 | × | 3 | = | |

(b)
| 5 | × | 3 | | |

(c)
| | | 3 | = | 6 |

(d)
| 9 | × | | | 27 |

(e)
| | | 3 | | 30 |

Revision 6

1.

(a)	(b)	(c)	(d)	(e)
0	7	3	9	1
× 6	× 6	× 6	× 6	× 8
___	___	___	___	___

2. Match.

× 6	
(a) 4•	•48
(b) 8•	•54
(c) 3•	•24
(d) 9•	•30
(e) 5•	•18

3. How many legs have…?

bee with 6 legs

(a) 3 bees = ____
(b) 7 bees = ____
(c) 2 bees = ____
(d) 8 bees = ____
(e) 4 bees = ____

4. Complete.

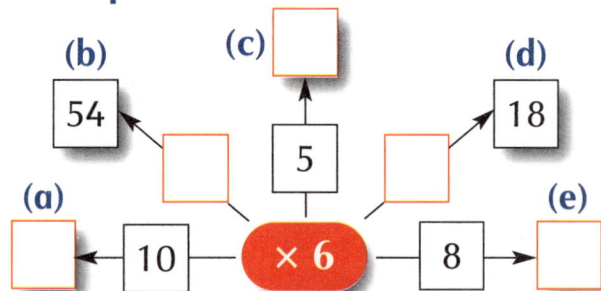

(a) ⬜ ← 10 ← × 6 → 8 → ⬜ (e)
(b) 54 ← ⬜
(c) ⬜ ↑ 5
(d) ⬜ → 18

5. ⭕> , ⭕< or ⭕=

(a) 5 × 6 ⭕ (6 + 6 + 6 + 6)
(b) 4 × 6 ⭕ 23
(c) 8 × 6 ⭕ (6 + 6 + 6 + 6 + 6)
(d) 9 × 6 ⭕ (8 × 6) + 7
(e) 7 × 6 ⭕ (6 × 6) + 8

Revision 7

1. Ring the **correct** answer.

(a) $7 \times 9 =$	54	63	36
(b) $5 \times 9 =$	32	45	54
(c) $0 \times 9 =$	1	9	0
(d) $6 \times 9 =$	54	60	72
(e) $8 \times 9 =$	56	72	76

2.

(a)	(b)	(c)	(d)	(e)
3	7	0	6	8
$\times 9$	$\times 9$	$\times 9$	$\times 9$	$\times 9$
——	——	——	——	——

3. How many **litres** in…?

9 litre

(a) 2 jars = ____ l

(b) 5 jars = ____ l

(c) 9 jars = ____ l

(d) 7 jars = ____ l

(e) 4 jars = ____ l

4.

(a)	(b)	(c)
☐	☐	☐
3 × 9	7 × 9	4 × 9

5. (a) (4×9) plus 6 = ____

(b) (6×9) minus 3 = ____

(c) (0×9) plus 12 = ____

(d) (8×9) minus 2 = ____

(e) (5×9) plus 7 = ____

(f) (7×9) add 2 = ____

(g) (9×9) minus 7 = ____

25

Revision 8

1.

(a)	(b)	(c)	(d)	(e)
4	6	7	10	8
$\times 3$	$\times 6$	$\times 9$	$\times 3$	$\times 6$
——	——	——	——	——

2. (a) 3, 6, ____, 12, ____, 18, ____.

(b) 12, 18, ____, 30, ____, ____, ____.

(c) 0, 9, ____, ____, 36, ____, ____.

(d) 12, 15, ____, 21, ____, ____, 30.

(e) 30, 36, ____, ____, ____, ____, 66.

3. Fill in the gaps.

(a) $\boxed{4} \times \bigcirc{9} \Rightarrow \Box + \bigcirc{5} = \Box$

(b) $\boxed{6} \times \bigcirc{3} \Rightarrow \Box - \bigcirc{4} = \Box$

(c) $\boxed{9} \times \bigcirc{6} \Rightarrow \Box + \bigcirc{6} = \Box$

(d) $\boxed{8} \times \bigcirc{3} \Rightarrow \Box - \bigcirc{7} = \Box$

(e) $\boxed{7} \times \bigcirc{9} \Rightarrow \Box - \bigcirc{9} = \Box$

4. (a) (7×3) minus 2 = ____

(b) (6×9) plus 5 = ____

(c) (8×6) minus 9 = ____

(d) (9×9) plus 8 = ____

(e) (7×6) minus 5 = ____

5. $>$, $<$ or $=$

(a) 6×3 ◯ $(3 + 3 + 3 + 3 + 3)$

(b) 5×6 ◯ 10×3

(c) 4×9 ◯ $(5 \times 9) - 10$

(d) 9×6 ◯ $(8 \times 6) + 7$

(e) 8×9 ◯ $(7 \times 9) + 10$

25

Record your **scores** on page **77.**

Count in 7s

0   7   14   21   28

Day 1   Say the tables.

	Learn these:
$0 \times 7 = 0$	$0 \times 7 = 0$
$1 \times 7 = 7$	
$2 \times 7 = 14$	
$3 \times 7 = 21$	
$4 \times 7 = 28$	
$5 \times 7 = 35$	$5 \times 7 = 35$
$6 \times 7 = 42$	
$7 \times 7 = 49$	
$8 \times 7 = 56$	
$9 \times 7 = 63$	
$10 \times 7 = 70$	$10 \times 7 = 70$
$11 \times 7 = 77$	
$12 \times 7 = 84$	

1. (a) $(7 + 7 + 7 + 7 + 7)$

    $\Rightarrow$ ____ $\times 7 =$ ____

   (b) $(10 + 10 + 10 + 10 + 10 + 10 + 10)$

    $\Rightarrow$ ____ $\times 7 =$ ____

2. (a) $(5 \times 7) + 7 =$ ____

   (b) $(10 \times 7) + 7 =$ ____

   (c) $(0 \times 7) + 7 =$ ____

   (d) $(10 \times 7) - 7 =$ ____

3. How many eyes have…?

7 eyes

   (a) 10 aliens = ____

   (b) 5 aliens = ____

   (c) 0 aliens = ____

4. (a) 5 groups of 7   = ____

   (b) 0 times 7   = ____

   (c) 10 groups of 7   = ____

   (d) 5 sets of 7   = ____

   (e) (0×7) plus 6   = ____

14

Day 2   Say the tables.

	Learn these:
$0 \times 7 = 0$	
$1 \times 7 = 7$	$1 \times 7 = 7$
$2 \times 7 = 14$	$2 \times 7 = 14$
$3 \times 7 = 21$	$3 \times 7 = 21$
$4 \times 7 = 28$	
$5 \times 7 = 35$	
$6 \times 7 = 42$	
$7 \times 7 = 49$	
$8 \times 7 = 56$	
$9 \times 7 = 63$	
$10 \times 7 = 70$	
$11 \times 7 = 77$	
$12 \times 7 = 84$	

1. (a) $1 \times 7 =$ ____   (d) $5 \times 7 =$ ____

   (b) $3 \times 7 =$ ____   (e) $2 \times 7 =$ ____

   (c) $10 \times 7 =$ ____   (f) $0 \times 7 =$ ____

2. (a) 7 $\Rightarrow$ (____ $\times 7$)   = ____

   (b) $(7 + 7)$ $\Rightarrow$ (____ $\times 7$)   = ____

   (c) $(7 + 7 + 7) \Rightarrow$ (____ $\times$ ____) = ____

3. Ring the correct answer.

(a) $3 \times 7 =$	14	21	28
(b) $2 \times 7 =$	7	14	16
(c) $10 \times 7 =$	70	77	84
(d) $1 \times 7 =$	0	7	1

4. Complete. (Multiply.)

(a) | 2 | × | 7 | = | |

(b) | | × | 7 | = | 21 |

(c) | | | 7 | = | 7 |

(d) | 5 | | | | 35 |

17

Day 3   Say the tables.

Learn these:

$0 \times 7 = 0$
$1 \times 7 = 7$
$2 \times 7 = 14$
$3 \times 7 = 21$
$4 \times 7 = 28$ $4 \times 7 = 28$
$5 \times 7 = 35$
$6 \times 7 = 42$ $6 \times 7 = 42$
$7 \times 7 = 49$
$8 \times 7 = 56$
$9 \times 7 = 63$ $9 \times 7 = 63$
$10 \times 7 = 70$
$11 \times 7 = 77$ $11 \times 7 = 77$
$12 \times 7 = 84$

1.
(a)	(b)	(c)	(d)	(e)
6	9	11	4	5
×7	×7	×7	×7	×7

2. **Find the cost of...**

€7

(a)   6 plants = €____
(b)   9 plants = €____
(c)   11 plants = €____
(d)   4 plants = €____

3. **Fill in the gaps.**

(a) $6 \times 7 \Rightarrow \boxed{} + 3 = \boxed{}$

(b) $11 \times 7 \Rightarrow \boxed{} - 6 = \boxed{}$

(c) $4 \times 7 \Rightarrow \boxed{} + 8 = \boxed{}$

(d) $9 \times 7 \Rightarrow \boxed{} - 4 = \boxed{}$

4. (a) (7 × 9) plus 2 = ____
   (b) (4 × 7) minus 4 = ____

15

Day 4   Say the tables.

Learn these:

$0 \times 7 = 0$
$1 \times 7 = 7$
$2 \times 7 = 14$
$3 \times 7 = 21$
$4 \times 7 = 28$
$5 \times 7 = 35$
$6 \times 7 = 42$
$7 \times 7 = 49$ $7 \times 7 = 49$
$8 \times 7 = 56$ $8 \times 7 = 56$
$9 \times 7 = 63$
$10 \times 7 = 70$
$11 \times 7 = 77$
$12 \times 7 = 84$ $12 \times 7 = 84$

1. **Fill in the gaps.**

(a) $\boxed{7} \quad ×7 \quad \boxed{} \quad -8 \quad \boxed{}$

(b) $\boxed{12} \quad ×7 \quad \boxed{} \quad +3 \quad \boxed{}$

(c) $\boxed{8} \quad ×7 \quad \boxed{} \quad +5 \quad \boxed{}$

(d) $\boxed{6} \quad ×7 \quad \boxed{} \quad -6 \quad \boxed{}$

(e) $\boxed{9} \quad ×7 \quad \boxed{} \quad -8 \quad \boxed{}$

2. **Complete.**

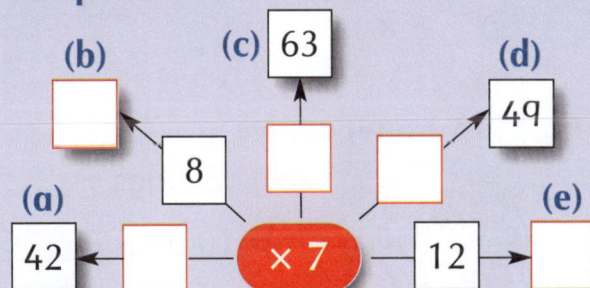

(b) □   (c) 63   (d) 49
8
(a) 42   × 7   12   (e)

3. (a) 21, 28, ____, ____, ____, 56, ____.
   (b) 7, 14, ____, ____, 35, ____, ____.
   (c) 49, 56, ____, ____, 77, ____.
   (d) 35, ____, 42, ____, 56, ____.

14

Do **Test 9** on page **62**.

Count in 11s

Day 1   Say the tables.

Learn these:

$0 \times 11 = 0$
$1 \times 11 = 11$
$2 \times 11 = 22$
$3 \times 11 = 33$
$4 \times 11 = 44$
$5 \times 11 = 55$
$6 \times 11 = 66$
$7 \times 11 = 77$
$8 \times 11 = 88$
$9 \times 11 = 99$
$10 \times 11 = 110$
$11 \times 11 = 121$
$12 \times 11 = 132$

Learn these:

$0 \times 11 = 0$

$5 \times 11 = 55$

$10 \times 11 = 110$

1. $(11 + 11 + 11 + 11 + 11)$

$\Rightarrow (\underline{\quad} \times 11) = \underline{\quad}$

2. **Complete. (Multiply.)**

(a) $\boxed{10} \times \boxed{11} = \boxed{}$

(b) $\boxed{} \times \boxed{11} = \boxed{0}$

(c) $\boxed{5} \ \boxed{} \ \boxed{} \ \boxed{55}$

3. (a) $0 \times 11 = \underline{\quad}$

(b) $11 \times 10 = \underline{\quad}$

(c) $5 \times 11 = \underline{\quad}$

(d)   (e)
0 11
$\times 11$ $\times 5$
___   ___

___   ___

4. **How many apples in…?**

(a) 5 bags = ___

(b) 10 bags = ___

(c) 0 bags = ___

11 apples

5. (a) $\underline{\quad} \times 11 = 110$

(b) $\underline{\quad} \times 5 = 55$

(c) $\underline{\quad} \times 11 = 0$

(d) $11 \times \underline{\quad} = 110$

16

Day 2   Say the tables.

Learn these:

$0 \times 11 = 0$
$1 \times 11 = 11$
$2 \times 11 = 22$
$3 \times 11 = 33$
$4 \times 11 = 44$
$5 \times 11 = 55$
$6 \times 11 = 66$
$7 \times 11 = 77$
$8 \times 11 = 88$
$9 \times 11 = 99$
$10 \times 11 = 110$
$11 \times 11 = 121$
$12 \times 11 = 132$

Learn these:

$1 \times 11 = 11$
$2 \times 11 = 22$
$3 \times 11 = 33$

1.
(a)	(b)	(c)	(d)	(e)
11	11	11	11	11
× 2	× 10	× 3	× 0	× 1
___	___	___	___	___
___	___	___	___	___

2. **How many players in…?**

(a) 1 team = ___

(b) 3 teams = ___

(c) 5 teams = ___

(d) 2 teams = ___

11 players

3. (a) $(2 \times 11) + 11 = \underline{\quad}$

(b) $(1 \times 11) + 11 = \underline{\quad}$

(c) $(0 \times 11) + 11 = \underline{\quad}$

(d) $(5 \times 11) - 11 = \underline{\quad}$

(e) $(3 \times 11) - 11 = \underline{\quad}$

4. (a) (2×11) plus 4 = ___

(b) (11×3) minus 6 = ___

(c) $\underline{\quad} \times 11 = 33$

17

Day 3   Say the tables.

Learn these:

0 × 11 = 0			
1 × 11 = 11			
2 × 11 = 22			
3 × 11 = 33			
4 × 11 = 44		4 × 11 = 44	
5 × 11 = 55			
6 × 11 = 66		6 × 11 = 66	
7 × 11 = 77			
8 × 11 = 88			
9 × 11 = 99		9 × 11 = 99	
10 × 11 = 110			
11 × 11 = 121		11 × 11 = 121	
12 × 11 = 132			

1. (a) (11 + 11 + 11 + 11)

⇒ ____ × 11 = ____

(b) (11 + 11 + 11 + 11 + 11 + 11)

⇒ ____ × 11 = ____

2. Ring the correct answer.

(a) 11 × 11 =	99	121	66
(b) 11 × 6 =	64	65	66
(c) 11 × 4 =	34	44	54
(d) 11 × 9 =	99	97	98

3. Complete.

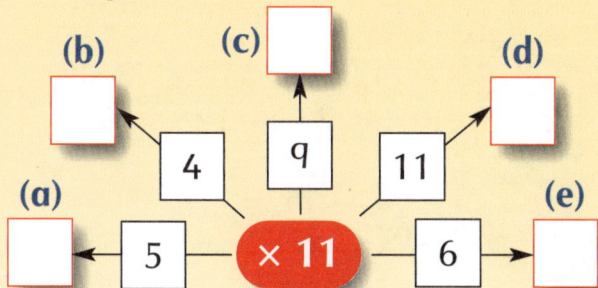

4. (11 + 11 + 11)

⇒ ____ × 11 = ____

12

Day 4   Say the tables.

Learn these:

0 × 11 = 0			
1 × 11 = 11			
2 × 11 = 22			
3 × 11 = 33			
4 × 11 = 44			
5 × 11 = 55			
6 × 11 = 66			
7 × 11 = 77		7 × 11 = 77	
8 × 11 = 88		8 × 11 = 88	
9 × 11 = 99			
10 × 11 = 110			
11 × 11 = 121			
12 × 11 = 132		12 × 11 = 132	

1. Fill in the gaps.

(a) 8 × 11 ☐ plus 6 ☐

(b) 12 × 11 ☐ minus 5 ☐

(c) 7 × 11 ☐ plus 8 ☐

(d) 9 × 11 ☐ minus 7 ☐

(e) 6 × 11 ☐ plus 4 ☐

2. Write the missing numbers.

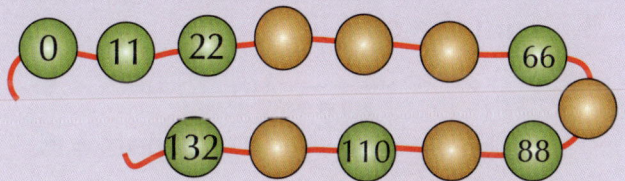

3. Factor boxes

(a) ☐ 11 / 33   (b) 5 ☐ / 55   (c) ☐ 11 / 77

(d) ☐ 11 / 88   (e) ☐ 12 / 132

☐ / 11

Do Test 10 on page 62.

25

Count in 12s

Day 1 — Say the tables.

	Learn these:
$0 \times 12 = 0$	$0 \times 12 = 0$
$1 \times 12 = 12$	
$2 \times 12 = 24$	
$3 \times 12 = 36$	
$4 \times 12 = 48$	
$5 \times 12 = 60$	$5 \times 12 = 60$
$6 \times 12 = 72$	
$7 \times 12 = 84$	
$8 \times 12 = 96$	
$9 \times 12 = 108$	
$10 \times 12 = 120$	$10 \times 12 = 120$
$11 \times 12 = 132$	
$12 \times 12 = 144$	

1.

(a)	(b)	(c)	(d)	(e)
0	5	10	12	12
$\times 12$	$\times 12$	$\times 12$	$\times 0$	$\times 5$
___	___	___	___	___

2. (a) $(12 + 12 + 12 + 12 + 12)$

   $\Rightarrow$ ____ $\times 12 =$ ____

   (b) $(12 + 12 + 12 + 12 + 12$
   $+ 12 + 12 + 12 + 12 + 12)$

   $\Rightarrow$ ____ $\times 12 =$ ____

3. Find the cost of…

   €12

   (a) 5 hats = € ____

   (b) 0 hats = € ____

   (c) 10 hats = € ____

4. ✔ or ✗

   (a) $0 \times 12 = 60$ ✗

   (b) $5 \times 12 = 60$ ☐

   (c) $10 \times 12 = 100$ ☐

   (d) $12 \times 0 = 120$ ☐

   13

Day 2 — Say the tables.

	Learn these:
$0 \times 12 = 0$	
$1 \times 12 = 12$	$1 \times 12 = 12$
$2 \times 12 = 24$	$2 \times 12 = 24$
$3 \times 12 = 36$	$3 \times 12 = 36$
$4 \times 12 = 48$	
$5 \times 12 = 60$	
$6 \times 12 = 72$	
$7 \times 12 = 84$	
$8 \times 12 = 96$	
$9 \times 12 = 108$	
$10 \times 12 = 120$	
$11 \times 12 = 132$	
$12 \times 12 = 144$	

1. (a) 0, 12, ____, ____, 48, ____.

   (b) 12, 24, ____, ____, 60, ____.

   (c) 24, 36, ____, ____, 72, ____.

2. Complete. (Multiply.)

   (a) | 2 | × | 12 | = | ☐ |

   (b) | ☐ | × | 12 | | 12 |

   (c) | 3 | | | = | 36 |

   (d) | ☐ | × | 12 | = | 60 |

3.

   (a) ☐ ⌃ 3 × 12

   (b) ☐ ⌃ 2 × 12

   (c) 120 ⌃ 12 × ☐

4. >, < or =

   (a) 3×12 ◯ 12×3

   (b) 2×12 ◯ 36

   (c) 12 ◯ 12×0

   13

Day 3　Say the tables.

Learn these:

$0 \times 12 = 0$
$1 \times 12 = 12$
$2 \times 12 = 24$
$3 \times 12 = 36$
$4 \times 12 = 48$　　$4 \times 12 = 48$
$5 \times 12 = 60$
$6 \times 12 = 72$　　$6 \times 12 = 72$
$7 \times 12 = 84$
$8 \times 12 = 96$
$9 \times 12 = 108$　　$9 \times 12 = 108$
$10 \times 12 = 120$
$11 \times 12 = 132$　　$11 \times 12 = 132$
$12 \times 12 = 144$

1. Match.

(a) 12×6 •　　　108

(b) 3×12 •　　　132

(c) 12×9 •　　　72

(d) 11×12 •　　　36

2. How many carriages have…?

train with 12 carriages

(a) 9 trains = ____
(b) 6 trains = ____
(c) 11 trains = ____
(d) 5 trains = ____
(e) 4 trains = ____

3.
(a) 4 groups of 12　　= ____
(b) 6 times 12　　　= ____
(c) 12 multiplied by 11 = ____
(d) 9 sets of 12　　　= ____
(e) (____ × 12) – 2 = 70
(f) (____ × 12) + 2 = 50

15

Day 4　Say the tables.

Learn these:

$0 \times 12 = 0$
$1 \times 12 = 12$
$2 \times 12 = 24$
$3 \times 12 = 36$
$4 \times 12 = 48$
$5 \times 12 = 60$
$6 \times 12 = 72$
$7 \times 12 = 84$　　$7 \times 12 = 84$
$8 \times 12 = 96$　　$8 \times 12 = 96$
$9 \times 12 = 108$
$10 \times 12 = 120$
$11 \times 12 = 132$
$12 \times 12 = 144$　　$12 \times 12 = 144$

1. Write the missing numbers.

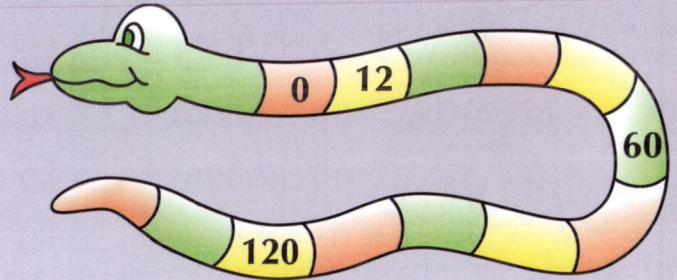

0　12　　60　120

2.
(a) $12 \times 7 =$ ____　(d) $11 \times 12 =$ ____
(b) $12 \times 4 =$ ____　(e) $12 \times 12 =$ ____
(c) $12 \times 0 =$ ____　(f) $8 \times 12 =$ ____

3. Factor boxes

(a) 9　12　　(b) ___　12 / 132　　(c) 8 / 96

4.
(a) $12 =$ ____ $\times 12$
(b) $96 =$ ____ $\times 12$
(c) $84 =$ ____ $\times 12$
(d) $144 =$ ____ $\times 12$

14

Do **Test 11** on page **63**.

Revision C — Multiplication by 7, 11 and 12

Revision 9

1. Match.

(a) 7 × 6 •

(b) 7 × 7 •

(c) 7 × 2 •

(d) 7 × 10 •

(e) 7 × 12 •

14
84
42
70
49

2. Factor boxes

(a) | 3 | 7 |

(b) | 7 | |
   | 28 | |

(c) | | 7 |
   | 63 | |

3. How many kg in…?

7kg

(a) 1 bag = ____kg

(b) 8 bags = ____kg

(c) 11 bags = ____kg

(d) 2 bags = ____kg

(e) 12 bags = ____kg

(f) 4 bags = ____kg

4.

(a)	(b)	(c)	(d)	(e)
7	9	0	4	12
× 7	× 7	× 7	× 7	× 7
___	___	___	___	___

5. (a) 14, 21, ____, ____, 42, ____, 56.

(b) 35, 42, ____, ____, 63, ____, 77.

6. Complete. (Multiply.)

(a) | 7 | × | 7 | = | |

(b) | 5 | × | 7 | | |

(c) | | | 7 | = | 77 |

(d) | 12 | | | | 84 |

25

Revision 10

1. Count on 11.

(a) | 11 | |

(b) | 99 | |

(c) | 55 | |

(d) | 33 | |

(e) | 0 | |

(f) | 110 | |

2. (a) 6 × 11 = ____

(b) 2 × 11 = ____

(c) 11 × 11 = ____

(d) 4 × 11 = ____

(e) 0 × 11 = ____

(f) 12 × 11 = ____

3. How many oranges are in…?

11 ORANGES

(a) 8 crates = ____

(b) 10 crates = ____

(c) 7 crates = ____

4. Factor boxes

(a) | 11 | |
   | 99 | |

(b) | | 11 |
   | 0 | |

(c) | | 1 |
   | 11 | |

5. (a) 22, 33, ____, ____, ____, 77.

(b) ____, 55, 66, ____, ____, 99.

6. Fill in the gaps.

(a) 9 ×11 → 99 +5 → ☐

(b) 4 ×11 → ☐ −3 → ☐

(c) 5 ×11 → ☐ +4 → ☐

(d) 6 ×11 → ☐ −8 → ☐

(e) 11 ×11 → ☐ +9 → ☐

25

Revision 11

1. How many buns on...?

(a) 4 trays = ____

(b) 2 trays = ____

(c) 7 trays = ____

tray of 12 buns

(d) 5 trays = ____

2. Match.

× 12	
(a) 11•	•132
(b) 4•	•108
(c) 6•	• 48
(d) 9•	• 72

3.

(a)	(b)	(c)	(d)	(e)
8	12	3	0	12
× 12	× 6	× 12	× 12	× 12
____	____	____	____	____

4. Match.

(a) 1 × 12 •

(b) 9 × 12 •

(c) 10 × 12 •

(d) 11 × 12 •

(e) 4 × 12 •

108
120
48
12
132

5. ✔ or ✗

(a) 0 × 12 = 60 ☐

(b) 6 × 12 = 72 ☐

(c) 10 × 12 = 110 ☐

(d) 9 × 12 = 98 ☐

6. (a) 12, ____, 36, ____, ____, 72.

(b) 60, ____, 84, ____, 108.

(c) ____, ____, ____, 36, 48.

25

Revision 12

1.

(a)	(b)	(c)	(d)	(e)
7	8	9	5	12
× 7	× 11	× 12	× 7	× 4
____	____	____	____	____
____	____	____	____	____

2. > , < or =

(a) 7 × 8 ◯ 4 × 11

(b) 11 × 3 ◯ 12 × 4

(c) 7 × 6 ◯ 48 − 6

(d) 7 × 4 ◯ 7 × 5

(e) 12 × 7 ◯ 8 × 11

3. (a) 7, 14, ____, ____, ____, 42.

(b) 11, 22, ____, 44, ____, ____.

(c) 12, 24, ____, 48, ____, ____.

4. Find the cost of...

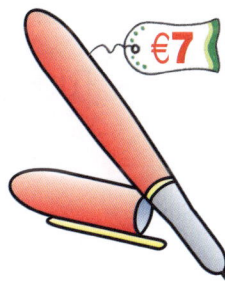

€7

(a) 3 pens = €____

(b) 4 pens = €____

(c) 5 pens = €____

(d) 8 pens = €____

(e) 9 pens = €____

(f) 10 pens = €____

5. (a) 4 groups of 7 = ____

(b) 6 times 11 = ____

(c) 12 multiplied by 11 = ____

(d) 9 sets of 12 = ____

(e) (____ × 12) − 2 = 70

(f) (____ × 11) + 7 = 73

25

▲ Record your scores on page 77.

Count in 10s

$$\boxed{0}\quad\boxed{10}\quad\boxed{20}\quad\boxed{30}\quad\boxed{40}$$

Day 1   Say the tables.

		Learn these:
$0 \div 10 = 0$		$0 \div 10 = 0$
$10 \div 10 = 1$		
$20 \div 10 = 2$		
$30 \div 10 = 3$		
$40 \div 10 = 4$		
$50 \div 10 = 5$		$50 \div 10 = 5$
$60 \div 10 = 6$		
$70 \div 10 = 7$		
$80 \div 10 = 8$		
$90 \div 10 = 9$		
$100 \div 10 = 10$		$100 \div 10 = 10$
$110 \div 10 = 11$		
$120 \div 10 = 12$		

1. (a) $0 \times 10 = 0$, so $0 \div 10 = \underline{\hspace{1cm}}$

  (b) $5 \times 10 = 50$, so $50 \div 10 = \underline{\hspace{1cm}}$

2.   (a) $5 \times 10 = \underline{\hspace{1cm}}$

       (b) $50 \div 10 = \underline{\hspace{1cm}}$

  (c) $\boxed{10}\ \boxed{10}\ \boxed{10}\ \boxed{10}\ \boxed{10} = \underline{\hspace{1cm}}$

     $5 \times 10 = \underline{\hspace{1cm}}$, so $50 \div 10 = \underline{\hspace{1cm}}$

3. Complete. (Divide.)

  (a) $\boxed{50}\ \boxed{\div}\ \boxed{10}\ \boxed{=}\ \boxed{}$

  (b) $\boxed{100}\ \boxed{}\ \boxed{}\ \boxed{=}\ \boxed{10}$

  (c) $\boxed{}\ \boxed{}\ \boxed{10}\ \boxed{}\ \boxed{0}$

4. Count back in 10s.

  $50 (-10 - 10 - 10 - 10 - 10) = 0$,

  so $50 \div 10 = \underline{\hspace{1cm}}$

5. (a) $10\,\overline{)50}$ (b) $10\,\overline{)100}$

      $\underline{\hspace{1cm}}$ $\underline{\hspace{1cm}}$ **11**

Day 2   Say the tables.

		Learn these:
$0 \div 10 = 0$		
$10 \div 10 = 1$		$10 \div 10 = 1$
$20 \div 10 = 2$		$20 \div 10 = 2$
$30 \div 10 = 3$		$30 \div 10 = 3$
$40 \div 10 = 4$		
$50 \div 10 = 5$		
$60 \div 10 = 6$		
$70 \div 10 = 7$		
$80 \div 10 = 8$		
$90 \div 10 = 9$		
$100 \div 10 = 10$		
$110 \div 10 = 11$		
$120 \div 10 = 12$		

1. (a) $10 \div 10 = \underline{\hspace{1cm}}$

  (b) $20 \div 10 = \underline{\hspace{1cm}}$

  (c) $30 \div 10 = \underline{\hspace{1cm}}$

2. How many **girls** make…?

10 toes

  (a) 20 toes = $\underline{\hspace{1cm}}$

  (b) 30 toes = $\underline{\hspace{1cm}}$

  (c) 10 toes = $\underline{\hspace{1cm}}$

3. (a) $1 \times 10 = 10$, so $10 \div 10 = \underline{\hspace{1cm}}$

  (b) $3 \times 10 = 30$, so $30 \div 10 = \underline{\hspace{1cm}}$

  (c) $2 \times 10 = 20$, so $\underline{\hspace{1cm}} \div 10 = 2$

4. (a) $10\,\overline{)10}$ (c) $10\,\overline{)30}$ (e) $10\,\overline{)20}$

      $\underline{\hspace{1cm}}$ $\underline{\hspace{1cm}}$ $\underline{\hspace{1cm}}$

  (b) $10\,\overline{)100}$ (d) $10\,\overline{)50}$

      $\underline{\hspace{1cm}}$ $\underline{\hspace{1cm}}$ **14**

Day 3   Say the tables.

				Learn these:
0	÷ 10 =	0		
10	÷ 10 =	1		
20	÷ 10 =	2		
30	÷ 10 =	3		
40	÷ 10 =	4		40 ÷ 10 = 4
50	÷ 10 =	5		
60	÷ 10 =	6		60 ÷ 10 = 6
70	÷ 10 =	7		
80	÷ 10 =	8		
90	÷ 10 =	9		90 ÷ 10 = 9
100	÷ 10 =	10		
110	÷ 10 =	11		110 ÷ 10 = 11
120	÷ 10 =	12		

1. How many stamps can I buy with…?

10c

(a) 40c = _____

(b) 90c = _____

(c) 60c = _____

(d) 110c = _____

2. (a) 9 × 10 = _____, so 90 ÷ 10 = _____

(b) 6 × 10 = _____, so _____ ÷ 10 = 6

(c) 4 × 10 = _____, so _____ ÷ 10 = 4

3. Factor boxes

(a) | 90 |
     | 10 | |

(b) | 110 |
     | 10 | |

(c) | 60 |
     | | 6 |

(d) | 40 |
     | | 4 |

(e) | 100 |
     | | 10 |

(f) | 50 |
     | | 5 |

4. (a) 60 ÷ 10 = _____

(b) 110 ÷ 10 = _____

(c) 40 ÷ 10 = _____

(d) 90 ÷ 10 = _____

| 17 |

Day 4   Say the tables.

				Learn these:
0	÷ 10 =	0		
10	÷ 10 =	1		
20	÷ 10 =	2		
30	÷ 10 =	3		
40	÷ 10 =	4		
50	÷ 10 =	5		
60	÷ 10 =	6		
70	÷ 10 =	7		70 ÷ 10 = 7
80	÷ 10 =	8		80 ÷ 10 = 8
90	÷ 10 =	9		
100	÷ 10 =	10		
110	÷ 10 =	11		
120	÷ 10 =	12		120 ÷ 10 = 12

1. How many boxes make…?

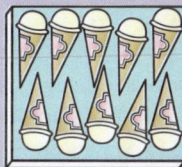

10 ice creams

(a) 70 ice creams = _____

(b) 120 ice creams = _____

(c) 80 ice creams = _____

2.

	(a)	(b)	(c)	(d)	(e)	(f)	(g)
÷	20	80	90	60	110	100	70
10							

3. Complete.

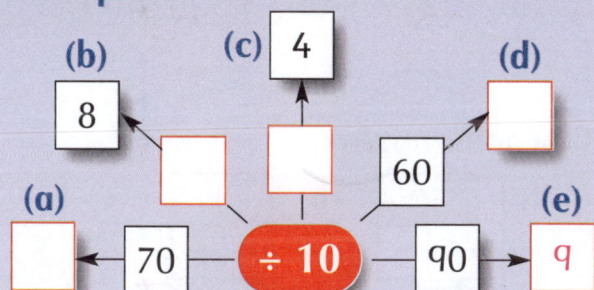

(b) 8

(c) 4

(d)

(a) _____ ← 70 ← ÷ 10 → 90 → (e) 9

60

4. (a) 10⟌70

(c) 10⟌_____
     4

(e) 10⟌60
     _____

(b) 10⟌_____
     1

(d) 10⟌120
     _____

| 19 |

Do **Test 12 on page 64**.

Count in 5s

Day 1　Say the tables.

				Learn these:
0	÷ 5 =	0		0 ÷ 5 = 0
5	÷ 5 =	1		
10	÷ 5 =	2		
15	÷ 5 =	3		
20	÷ 5 =	4		
25	÷ 5 =	5		25 ÷ 5 = 5
30	÷ 5 =	6		
35	÷ 5 =	7		
40	÷ 5 =	8		
45	÷ 5 =	9		
50	÷ 5 =	10		50 ÷ 5 = 10
55	÷ 5 =	11		
60	÷ 5 =	12		

1.　(a)　5×5 = ____
　(b)　$25 \div 5$ = ____

　(c)　10×5 = ____
　(d)　$50 \div 5$ = ____
　(e)　$50 \div 10$ = ____
　(f)　5×10 = ____

　(g)　$0 \div 5$ = ____

2.　(a) 5⟌25　(b) 5⟌50　(c) 5⟌0
　　 ____　　 ____　　 ____

3. Factor boxes

　(a) 50 / 5 __　(b) 0 __ / __ 5　(c) 25 __ / 5 __

4.　(a) $\dfrac{50}{5}$ = ___　(b) $\dfrac{25}{5}$ = ___

5.　$25 (-5-5-5-5-5)$ = ____,
　　so $25 \div 5$ = ____

16

Day 2　Say the tables.

				Learn these:
0	÷ 5 =	0		
5	÷ 5 =	1		5 ÷ 5 = 1
10	÷ 5 =	2		10 ÷ 5 = 2
15	÷ 5 =	3		15 ÷ 5 = 3
20	÷ 5 =	4		
25	÷ 5 =	5		
30	÷ 5 =	6		
35	÷ 5 =	7		
40	÷ 5 =	8		
45	÷ 5 =	9		
50	÷ 5 =	10		
55	÷ 5 =	11		
60	÷ 5 =	12		

1.　(a)　$10 \div 5$ = ____

　(b)　$15 \div 5$ = ____

2.　(a)　$1 \times 5 = 5$,　so　$5 \div 5$ = ____
　(b)　3×5 = ____, so $15 \div 5$ = ____
　(c)　2×5 = ____, so $10 \div$ ____ = 2

3. How many bags make…?

　(a)　15 nuts = ____
　(b)　25 nuts = ____
　(c)　10 nuts = ____

bag of 5 nuts

4.　(a) 5⟌10　(c) 5⟌15　(e) 5⟌5
　　 ____　　 ____　　 ____

　(b) 5⟌25　(d) 5⟌0　(f) 5⟌50
　　 ____　　 ____　　 ____

5.　(a) $\dfrac{10}{5}$ = ____　(b) $\dfrac{5}{5}$ = ____

16

Day 3 — Say the tables.

Learn these:

$0 \div 5 = 0$
$5 \div 5 = 1$
$10 \div 5 = 2$
$15 \div 5 = 3$
$20 \div 5 = 4$ $20 \div 5 = 4$
$25 \div 5 = 5$
$30 \div 5 = 6$ $30 \div 5 = 6$
$35 \div 5 = 7$
$40 \div 5 = 8$
$45 \div 5 = 9$ $45 \div 5 = 9$
$50 \div 5 = 10$
$55 \div 5 = 11$ $55 \div 5 = 11$
$60 \div 5 = 12$

1. Count back in 5s.

(a) $20 (- 5 - 5 - 5 - 5) = $ _____,

so $20 \div 5 = $ ____

(b) $30 (- 5 - 5 - 5 - 5 - 5 - 5) = $ _____,

so $30 \div 5 = $ ____

2.

(a) $9 \times 5 = $ ____
(b) $45 \div 5 = $ ____
(c) $45 \div 9 = $ ____
(d) $11 \times 5 = $ ____
(e) $55 \div 5 = $ ____
(f) $55 \div 11 = $ ____

3. Factor boxes

(a) | 45 |
    | 5 | |

(b) | 25 |
    | 5 | |

(c) | 30 |
    | 5 | |

(d) | 20 |
    | 5 | |

(e) | 15 |
    | 5 | |

(f) | 55 |
    | 5 | |

4. (a) $5\overline{)45}$ (b) $5\overline{)30}$

____   ____

16

Day 4 — Say the tables.

Learn these:

$0 \div 5 = 0$
$5 \div 5 = 1$
$10 \div 5 = 2$
$15 \div 5 = 3$
$20 \div 5 = 4$
$25 \div 5 = 5$
$30 \div 5 = 6$
$35 \div 5 = 7$ $35 \div 5 = 7$
$40 \div 5 = 8$ $40 \div 5 = 8$
$45 \div 5 = 9$
$50 \div 5 = 10$
$55 \div 5 = 11$
$60 \div 5 = 12$ $60 \div 5 = 12$

1. (a) $7 \times 5 = $ ____, so $35 \div 5 = $ ____

(b) $12 \times 5 = $ ____, so $60 \div 5 = $ ____

(c) $8 \times 5 = $ ____, so $40 \div 5 = $ ____

2. How many starfish make…?

(a) 35 legs = ____
(b) 40 legs = ____
(c) 45 legs = ____

star fish with 5 legs   (d) 20 legs = ____

3. Complete.

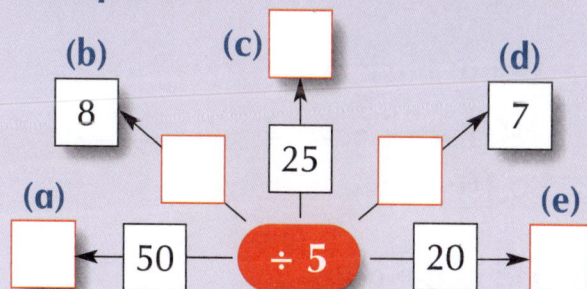

4. (a) $(40 \div 5) + 4 = $ ____

(b) $(35 \div 5) - 2 = $ ____

(c) $(60 \div 5) - 6 = $ ____

15

Do Test 13 on page 64.

Count in 2s

0 2 4 6 8

Day 1 Say the tables.

	Learn these:
$0 \div 2 = 0$	$0 \div 2 = 0$
$2 \div 2 = 1$	
$4 \div 2 = 2$	
$6 \div 2 = 3$	
$8 \div 2 = 4$	
$10 \div 2 = 5$	$10 \div 2 = 5$
$12 \div 2 = 6$	
$14 \div 2 = 7$	
$16 \div 2 = 8$	
$18 \div 2 = 9$	
$20 \div 2 = 10$	$20 \div 2 = 10$
$22 \div 2 = 11$	
$24 \div 2 = 12$	

1. (a) ⬛⬛⬛⬛⬛⬛⬛⬛⬛⬛ $20 \div 2 = $ ____

   (b) ⬛⬛⬛⬛⬛ $10 \div 2 = $ ____

2. **How many planes make…?**

   plane with 2 wings

   (a) 10 wings = ____

   (b) 20 wings = ____

   (c) 0 wings = ____

3. (a) $10 \times 2 = 20$, so $20 \div 2 = $ ____

   (b) $5 \times 2 = $ ____, so $10 \div 2 = $ ____

   (c) $0 \times 2 = $ ____, so $0 \div 2 = $ ____

4. **Count back in 2s.**

   $10 (- 2 - 2 - 2 - 2 - 2) = $ ____,

   so $10 \div 2 = $ ____

5. **Fill in the gaps.**

   (a) 10 ÷2 → 5 +4 → ☐

   (b) 20 ÷2 → ☐ ÷2 → ☐

   (c) 0 ÷2 → ☐ +2 → ☐

   12

Day 2 Say the tables.

	Learn these:
$0 \div 2 = 0$	
$2 \div 2 = 1$	$2 \div 2 = 1$
$4 \div 2 = 2$	$4 \div 2 = 2$
$6 \div 2 = 3$	$6 \div 2 = 3$
$8 \div 2 = 4$	
$10 \div 2 = 5$	
$12 \div 2 = 6$	
$14 \div 2 = 7$	
$16 \div 2 = 8$	
$18 \div 2 = 9$	
$20 \div 2 = 10$	
$22 \div 2 = 11$	
$24 \div 2 = 12$	

1. **How many bicycles make…?**

   bicycle with 2 wheels

   (a) 4 wheels = ____

   (b) 6 wheels = ____

   (c) 2 wheels = ____

2. (a) $4 \div 2 = $ ____

   (b) $6 \div 2 = $ ____

3. (a) $2\overline{)2}$ (c) $2\overline{)4}$ (e) $2\overline{)6}$

   (b) $2\overline{)10}$ (d) $2\overline{)20}$ (f) $2\overline{)0}$

4. (a) $6 \div 2 = $ ____, so ____ $\times 2 = 6$

   (b) $4 \div 2 = $ ____, so $2 \times 2 = $ ____

   (c) $2 \div 2 = $ ____, so ____ $\times 2 = 2$

5. (a) $\dfrac{4}{2} = $ ____ (c) $\dfrac{2}{2} = $ ____

   (b) $\dfrac{6}{2} = $ ____ (d) $\dfrac{0}{2} = $ ____

   18

Day 3   Say the tables.

Learn these:

$0 \div 2 = 0$
$2 \div 2 = 1$
$4 \div 2 = 2$
$6 \div 2 = 3$
$8 \div 2 = 4$ $8 \div 2 = 4$
$10 \div 2 = 5$
$12 \div 2 = 6$ $12 \div 2 = 6$
$14 \div 2 = 7$
$16 \div 2 = 8$
$18 \div 2 = 9$ $18 \div 2 = 9$
$20 \div 2 = 10$
$22 \div 2 = 11$ $22 \div 2 = 11$
$24 \div 2 = 12$

1. (a) $22 \div 2 =$ _____

(b) $18 \div 2 =$ _____

2. (a) $2\,|\,8$ (c) $2\,|\,12$ (e) $2\,|\,18$
___   ___   ___

(b) $2\,|\,20$ (d) $2\,|\,10$ (f) $2\,|\,22$
___   ___   ___

3. Fill in the gaps.

(a) $6 \div 2 \Rightarrow 3 + 5 = \boxed{}$

(b) $18 \div 2 \Rightarrow \boxed{} - 3 = \boxed{}$

(c) $4 \div 2 \Rightarrow \boxed{} + 7 = \boxed{}$

(d) $22 \div 2 \Rightarrow \boxed{} - 4 = \boxed{}$

(e) $12 \div 2 \Rightarrow \boxed{} + 2 = \boxed{}$

4. (a) $(18 \div 2)$ minus $3 =$ _____

(b) $(6 \div 2)$ plus $2 =$ _____

(c) $(22 \div 2)$ plus $4 =$ _____

16

Day 4   Say the tables.

Learn these:

$0 \div 2 = 0$
$2 \div 2 = 1$
$4 \div 2 = 2$
$6 \div 2 = 3$
$8 \div 2 = 4$
$10 \div 2 = 5$
$12 \div 2 = 6$
$14 \div 2 = 7$ $14 \div 2 = 7$
$16 \div 2 = 8$ $16 \div 2 = 8$
$18 \div 2 = 9$
$20 \div 2 = 10$
$22 \div 2 = 11$
$24 \div 2 = 12$ $24 \div 2 = 12$

1. Factor boxes

(a) $\boxed{}$ (b) $\boxed{16}$ (c) $\boxed{24}$
$\boxed{7}\ \boxed{2}$ $\boxed{}\ \boxed{2}$ $\boxed{}\ \boxed{2}$

2. How many rabbits make…?

(a) 16 ears = _____

(b) 14 ears = _____

(c) 24 ears = _____

rabbit with 2 ears

3.   (a) $14 \div 7 =$ _____

(b) $14 \div 2 =$ _____

4. (a) $2\,|\,14$ (b) $2\,|\,16$ (c) $2\,|\,24$
___   ___   ___

5. (a) $(14 \div 2)$ plus $8 =$ _____

(b) $(16 \div 2)$ minus $3 =$ _____

(c) $(24 \div 2)$ plus $6 =$ _____

(d) $(12 \div 2) + 4 =$ _____

(e) $(18 \div 2) - 3 =$ _____

16

Do **Test 14** on page **65**.

Count in 4s

$$0 \quad 4 \quad 8 \quad 12 \quad 16$$

Day 1   Say the tables.

Learn these:

$0 \div 4 = 0$		$0 \div 4 = 0$
$4 \div 4 = 1$		
$8 \div 4 = 2$		
$12 \div 4 = 3$		
$16 \div 4 = 4$		
$20 \div 4 = 5$		$20 \div 4 = 5$
$24 \div 4 = 6$		
$28 \div 4 = 7$		
$32 \div 4 = 8$		
$36 \div 4 = 9$		
$40 \div 4 = 10$		$40 \div 4 = 10$
$44 \div 4 = 11$		
$48 \div 4 = 12$		

1.

(a) $20 \div 4 = \underline{\quad}$

(b) $20 \div 5 = \underline{\quad}$

(c) $40 \div 4 = \underline{\quad}$

(d) $40 \div 10 = \underline{\quad}$

2. How many ponies make…?

(a) 20 legs $= \underline{\quad}$

(b) 40 legs $= \underline{\quad}$

(c) 0 legs $= \underline{\quad}$

horse with 4 legs

3. (a) $0 \times 4 = \underline{\quad}$, so $0 \div 4 = \underline{\quad}$

(b) $10 \times 4 = \underline{\quad}$, so $\underline{\quad} \div 4 = 10$

(c) $5 \times \underline{\quad} = 20$, so $20 \div 4 = \underline{\quad}$

4. (a) $4\overline{)40}$ (b) $4\overline{)20}$ (c) $4\overline{)0}$

5. Complete. (Divide.)

(a)

20	÷	4	=	

(b)

40			=	10

15

Day 2   Say the tables.

Learn these:

$0 \div 4 = 0$		
$4 \div 4 = 1$		$4 \div 4 = 1$
$8 \div 4 = 2$		$8 \div 4 = 2$
$12 \div 4 = 3$		$12 \div 4 = 3$
$16 \div 4 = 4$		
$20 \div 4 = 5$		
$24 \div 4 = 6$		
$28 \div 4 = 7$		
$32 \div 4 = 8$		
$36 \div 4 = 9$		
$40 \div 4 = 10$		
$44 \div 4 = 11$		
$48 \div 4 = 12$		

1. How many cats make…?

cat with 4 legs

(a) 4 legs $= \underline{\quad}$

(b) 8 legs $= \underline{\quad}$

(c) 12 legs $= \underline{\quad}$

2. (a) $1 \times 4 = \underline{\quad}$, so $\underline{\quad} \div 4 = 1$

(b) $3 \times 4 = \underline{\quad}$, so $\underline{\quad} \div 4 = 3$

(c) $2 \times 4 = \underline{\quad}$, so $\underline{\quad} \div 4 = 2$

3. Factor boxes

(a)

20	
4	

(b)

12	
4	

(c)

8	
4	

4.

(a) $8 \div 4 = \underline{\quad}$

(b) $8 \div 2 = \underline{\quad}$

5. (a) $\dfrac{12}{4} = \underline{\quad}$ (b) $\dfrac{8}{4} = \underline{\quad}$

6. (a) $(8 \div 4)$ minus 2 $= \underline{\quad}$

(b) $(12 \div 4)$ plus 6 $= \underline{\quad}$

(c) $(40 \div 4)$ minus 7 $= \underline{\quad}$

16

Day 3   Say the tables.

0	÷	4	=	0
4	÷	4	=	1
8	÷	4	=	2
12	÷	4	=	3
16	÷	4	=	4
20	÷	4	=	5
24	÷	4	=	6
28	÷	4	=	7
32	÷	4	=	8
36	÷	4	=	9
40	÷	4	=	10
44	÷	4	=	11
48	÷	4	=	12

Learn these:

$16 ÷ 4 = 4$

$24 ÷ 4 = 6$

$36 ÷ 4 = 9$

$44 ÷ 4 = 11$

1. Count back in 4s.

(a) $16 (– 4 – 4 – 4 – 4) = 0$,

so $16 ÷ 4 =$ _____

(b) $24 (– 4 – 4 – 4 – 4 – 4 – 4) =$ _____,

so $24 ÷ 4 =$ _____

2. (a) $11 × 4 =$ _____, so _____ $÷ 4 = 11$

(b) $9 × 4 =$ _____, so _____ $÷ 4 = 9$

3. How many scarves can I buy with…?

€4

(a) €36 = _____

(b) €24 = _____

(c) €16 = _____

(d) €44 = _____

4. Fill in the gaps.

(a) 24 ÷ 4 [ ] – 4 [ ]

(b) 44 ÷ 4 [ ] + 4 [ ]

(c) 36 ÷ 4 [ ] – 4 [ ]

11

Day 4   Say the tables.

0	÷	4	=	0
4	÷	4	=	1
8	÷	4	=	2
12	÷	4	=	3
16	÷	4	=	4
20	÷	4	=	5
24	÷	4	=	6
28	÷	4	=	7
32	÷	4	=	8
36	÷	4	=	9
40	÷	4	=	10
44	÷	4	=	11
48	÷	4	=	12

Learn these:

$28 ÷ 4 = 7$

$32 ÷ 4 = 8$

$48 ÷ 4 = 12$

1. (a) $7 × 4 =$ _____, so _____ $÷ 4 = 7$

(b) $12 × 4 =$ _____, so _____ $÷ 4 = 12$

(c) $8 × 4 =$ _____, so _____ $÷ 4 =$ _____

2. How many cars make…?

car with 4 wheels

(a) 32 wheels = _____

(b) 28 wheels = _____

(c) 36 wheels = _____

(d) 48 wheels = _____

(e) 24 wheels = _____

3. Factor boxes

(a) 28 / 4 [ ]   (b) 24 / 4 [ ]   (c) 32 / 4 [ ]

4. (a) 4|12   (b) 4|36   (c) 4|40

(d) 4|16   (e) 4|24   (f) 4|28

5. (32 divided by 4) plus 3 = _____

18

Do **Test 15** on page **65**.

Count in 8s

Day 1 — Say the tables.

					Learn these:
0	÷	8	=	0	$0 \div 8 = 0$
8	÷	8	=	1	
16	÷	8	=	2	
24	÷	8	=	3	
32	÷	8	=	4	
40	÷	8	=	5	$40 \div 8 = 5$
48	÷	8	=	6	
56	÷	8	=	7	
64	÷	8	=	8	
72	÷	8	=	9	
80	÷	8	=	10	$80 \div 8 = 10$
88	÷	8	=	11	
96	÷	8	=	12	

1. (a) $0 \times 8 = \underline{\quad}$, so $\underline{\quad} \div 8 = 0$

   (b) $5 \times 8 = \underline{\quad}$, so $\underline{\quad} \div 8 = 5$

   (c) $10 \times 8 = \underline{\quad}$, so $\underline{\quad} \div 8 = 10$

2. Count back in 8s.

   $40 (-8 - 8 - 8 - 8 - 8) = 0$,

   so $40 \div 8 = \underline{\quad}$

3. (a) $8\overline{)40}$ (b) $8\overline{)80}$ (c) $8\overline{)0}$

4. Complete. (Divide.)

   (a) | 40 | ÷ | 8 | = | |

   (b) | 0 | ÷ | 8 | | |

   (c) | | | 8 | = | 10 |

5. (a) $(40 \div 8)$ plus 6 $= \underline{\quad}$

   (b) $(80 \div 8)$ minus 7 $= \underline{\quad}$

   (c) $(0 \div 8)$ plus 5 $= \underline{\quad}$ 14

   (d) (40 divided by 8) $= \underline{\quad}$

Day 2 — Say the tables.

					Learn these:
0	÷	8	=	0	
8	÷	8	=	1	$8 \div 8 = 1$
16	÷	8	=	2	$16 \div 8 = 2$
24	÷	8	=	3	$24 \div 8 = 3$
32	÷	8	=	4	
40	÷	8	=	5	
48	÷	8	=	6	
56	÷	8	=	7	
64	÷	8	=	8	
72	÷	8	=	9	
80	÷	8	=	10	
88	÷	8	=	11	
96	÷	8	=	12	

1. (a) $8 \div 8 = \underline{\quad}$

   (b) $16 \div 8 = \underline{\quad}$

   (c) $24 \div 8 = \underline{\quad}$

2. (a) $1 \times 8 = \underline{\quad}$, so $\underline{\quad} \div 8 = 1$

   (b) $3 \times 8 = \underline{\quad}$, so $\underline{\quad} \div 8 = 3$

   (c) $2 \times 8 = \underline{\quad}$, so $\underline{\quad} \div 8 = 2$

3. How many trays hold…?

   tray of 8 buns

   (a) 16 buns = $\underline{\quad}$

   (b) 24 buns = $\underline{\quad}$

   (c) 8 buns = $\underline{\quad}$

   (d) 40 buns = $\underline{\quad}$

   (e) 80 buns = $\underline{\quad}$

4. (a) $8\overline{)80}$ (c) $8\overline{)40}$ (e) $8\overline{)24}$

   (b) $8\overline{)16}$ (d) $8\overline{)8}$ 16

Day 3   Say the tables.

Learn these:

0 ÷ 8 =	0		
8 ÷ 8 =	1		
16 ÷ 8 =	2		
24 ÷ 8 =	3		
32 ÷ 8 =	4	32 ÷ 8 =	4
40 ÷ 8 =	5		
48 ÷ 8 =	6	48 ÷ 8 =	6
56 ÷ 8 =	7		
64 ÷ 8 =	8		
72 ÷ 8 =	9	72 ÷ 8 =	9
80 ÷ 8 =	10		
88 ÷ 8 =	11	88 ÷ 8 =	11
96 ÷ 8 =	12		

1. (a) $9 \times 8 = $ _____, so _____ $\div 8 = $ _____

   (b) $11 \times 8 = $ _____, so _____ $\div 8 = $ _____

2. (a) $32 \div 8 = $ _____

   (b) $72 \div 8 = $ _____

   (c) $48 \div 8 = $ _____

   (d) $88 \div 8 = $ _____

3. (a) $\dfrac{32}{8} = $ _____ (c) $\dfrac{72}{8} = $ _____

   (b) $\dfrac{88}{8} = $ _____ (d) $\dfrac{48}{8} = $ _____

4. **Fill in the gaps.**

   (a) 32 ÷ 8 ▶ ☐ − 1 ▶ ☐

   (b) 48 ÷ 8 ▶ ☐ + 7 ▶ ☐

   (c) 72 ÷ 8 ▶ ☐ − 3 ▶ ☐

   (d) 88 ÷ 8 ▶ ☐ + 6 ▶ ☐

   14

Day 4   Say the tables.

Learn these:

0 ÷ 8 =	0		
8 ÷ 8 =	1		
16 ÷ 8 =	2		
24 ÷ 8 =	3		
32 ÷ 8 =	4		
40 ÷ 8 =	5		
48 ÷ 8 =	6		
56 ÷ 8 =	7	56 ÷ 8 =	7
64 ÷ 8 =	8	64 ÷ 8 =	8
72 ÷ 8 =	9		
80 ÷ 8 =	10		
88 ÷ 8 =	11		
96 ÷ 8 =	12	96 ÷ 8 =	12

1. **Complete.**

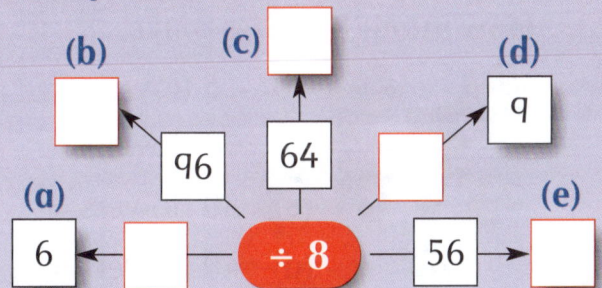

2. (a) $7 \times 8 = $ _____, so _____ $\div 8 = 7$

   (b) $12 \times 8 = $ _____, so _____ $\div 8 = 12$

   (c) $8 \times 8 = $ _____, so _____ $\div 8 = 8$

   (d) $9 \times 8 = $ _____, so _____ $\div 8 = 9$

3. **Factor boxes**

   (a) | 64 | |
       |---|---|
       | 8 | |

   (b) | 56 | |
       |---|---|
       | 8 | |

   (c) | 96 | |
       |---|---|
       | 8 | |

4. (a) $56 \div 8 = $ _____ (b) $64 \div 8 = $ _____

5. (a) $(96 \div 8) + 9 = $ _____

   (b) $(72 \div 8) - 6 = $ _____

   16

Do **Test 16** on page **66**.

Revision D   Division by 10, 5, 2, 4 and 8

Revision 13

1. (a) $10\overline{)100}$ (d) $5\overline{)20}$

    (b) $5\overline{)35}$ (e) $10\overline{)20}$

    (c) $10\overline{)90}$ (f) $5\overline{)45}$

2. Complete.

(b) 11   (c) ☐   (d) 8

(a) 4   ☐   30   ☐   (e)

÷ 10   20 → ☐

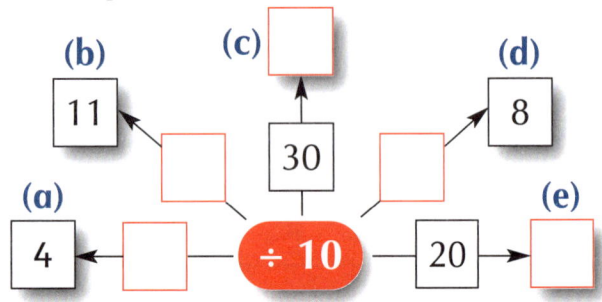

3. How many **bunches** make…?

(a) 5 flowers = ____

(b) 10 flowers = ____

(c) 30 flowers = ____

(d) 40 flowers = ____

(e) 55 flowers = ____

bunch of 5 flowers

4. Fill in the gaps.

(a) $40 \div 10 \Rightarrow \boxed{} + 7 = \boxed{}$

(b) $25 \div 5 \Rightarrow \boxed{} - 4 = \boxed{}$

(c) $70 \div 10 \Rightarrow \boxed{} - 3 = \boxed{}$

(d) $40 \div 5 \Rightarrow \boxed{} + 9 = \boxed{}$

(e) $45 \div 5 \Rightarrow \boxed{} - 3 = \boxed{}$

5. (a) $(35 \div 5)$ plus 8   = ____

   (b) $(80 \div 10)$ minus 4 = ____

   (c) $(50 \div 10)$ minus 5 = ____

   (d) $(55 \div 5)$ plus 6   = ____

25

Revision 14

1. How many **bags** hold…?

(a) 2 sweets = ____

(b) 4 sweets = ____

(c) 6 sweets = ____

(d) 10 sweets = ____

(e) 12 sweets = ____

2 sweets in a bag

2. (a) $18 \div 2 =$ ____

   (b) $4 \div 2 =$ ____

   (c) $10 \div 2 =$ ____

   (d) $0 \div 2 =$ ____

   (e) $14 \div 2 =$ ____

   (f) $24 \div 2 =$ ____

3. (a) $2\overline{)10}$ (d) $2\overline{)8}$

   (b) $2\overline{)2}$ (e) $2\overline{)16}$

   (c) $2\overline{)20}$ (f) $2\overline{)18}$

4. (a) 10 → ☐ × 5   (b) 22 → ☐ × 2   (c) 24 → ☐ × 2

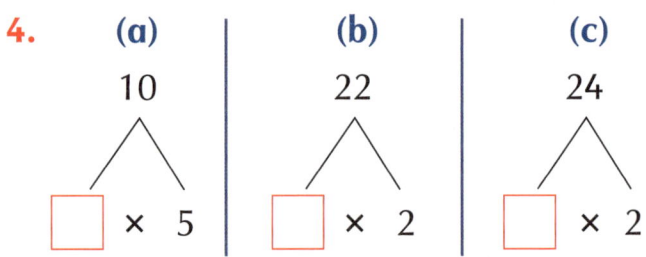

5. Complete. (**Divide.**)

(a) $8 \div 2 =$ ☐

(b) $12 \quad 2 =$ ☐

(c) $16 \quad = 8$

(d) ☐ $\div 2 \quad 10$

(e) $24 \quad 12$

25

Revision 15

1. (a) $32 \div 4 =$ _____

(b) $16 \div 4 =$ _____

(c) $4 \div 4 =$ _____

(d) $48 \div 4 =$ _____

(e) $28 \div 4 =$ _____

(f) $24 \div 4 =$ _____

2. Fill in the gaps.

(a) 20 → ÷4 → ☐ → +7 → ☐

(b) 16 → ÷4 → ☐ → −2 → ☐

(c) 24 → ÷4 → ☐ → −5 → ☐

(d) 32 → ÷4 → ☐ → ÷4 → ☐

(e) 48 → ÷4 → ☐ → ÷4 → ☐

3.

	(a)	(b)	(c)	(d)	(e)
÷	4	20	28		44
4				9	

4. How many balls can I buy with…?

€4

(a) €8 = _____

(b) €36 = _____

(c) €44 = _____

(d) €12 = _____

(e) €20 = _____

5. (a) $(28 \div 4)$ plus 8 = _____

(b) $(8 \div 4)$ minus 2 = _____

(c) $(32 \div 4)$ plus 4 = _____

(d) $(24 \div 4)$ minus 3 = _____

25

Revision 16

1. (a) $8\overline{)88}$ (d) $8\overline{)16}$

(b) $8\overline{)72}$ (e) $8\overline{)40}$

(c) $8\overline{)8}$ (f) $8\overline{)48}$

2. How many boxes can I buy with…?

€8

(a) €8 = _____

(b) €64 = _____

(c) €16 = _____

(d) €32 = _____

3. Factor boxes

(a) 64 / 8 ☐ (b) 24 / 3 ☐ (c) 40 / 8 ☐

(d) 56 / ☐ 8 (e) 80 / 10 ☐ (f) 8 / 8 ☐

4. Complete. (Divide.)

(a) | 40 | ÷ | 8 | = | ☐ |

(b) | 56 | | | = | 7 |

(c) | | | 8 | = | 8 |

(d) | 72 | ÷ | | | 9 |

5. (a) $\dfrac{32}{8} =$ _____ (d) $\dfrac{48}{8} =$ _____

(b) $\dfrac{64}{8} =$ _____ (e) $\dfrac{72}{8} =$ _____

(c) $\dfrac{16}{8} =$ _____

25

Record your scores on page 77.

41

Count in 3s

| 0 | 3 | 6 | 9 | 12 |

Day 1   Say the tables.

Learn these:

0	÷	3	=	0		
3	÷	3	=	1		
6	÷	3	=	2		
9	÷	3	=	3		
12	÷	3	=	4		
15	÷	3	=	5		
18	÷	3	=	6		
21	÷	3	=	7		
24	÷	3	=	8		
27	÷	3	=	9		
30	÷	3	=	10		
33	÷	3	=	11		
36	÷	3	=	12		

Learn these (Day 1):
$0 ÷ 3 = 0$
$15 ÷ 3 = 5$
$30 ÷ 3 = 10$

1. (a) $15 ÷ 3 = $ ____

(b) $30 ÷ 3 = $ ____

2. (a) $10 × 3 = 30$, so $30 ÷ 3 = $ ____

(b) $5 × 3 = 15$, so $15 ÷ 3 = $ ____

(c) $0 × 3 = 0$, so $0 ÷ 3 = $ ____

3. (a) $3\overline{)30}$ (b) $3\overline{)15}$ (c) $3\overline{)0}$

4. Factor boxes

(a) | 0 | | (b) | 30 | | (c) | 15 | |
    | 3 | | | | 3 | | | 3 |

5. (a) 30 shared among 3 = ____

(b) 0 divided by 3 = ____

(c) $(30 ÷ 3) − 7$ = ____

(d) $(15 ÷ 3) + 6$ = ____

(e) $(0 ÷ 3) × 3$ = ____ | 16 |

Day 2   Say the tables.

Learn these:

0	÷	3	=	0		
3	÷	3	=	1		
6	÷	3	=	2		
9	÷	3	=	3		
12	÷	3	=	4		
15	÷	3	=	5		
18	÷	3	=	6		
21	÷	3	=	7		
24	÷	3	=	8		
27	÷	3	=	9		
30	÷	3	=	10		
33	÷	3	=	11		
36	÷	3	=	12		

Learn these (Day 2):
$3 ÷ 3 = 1$
$6 ÷ 3 = 2$
$9 ÷ 3 = 3$

1. (a) $3 ÷ 3 = $ ____

(b) $6 ÷ 3 = $ ____

(c) $9 ÷ 3 = $ ____

2. How many bags hold…?

3 marbles

(a) 3 marbles = ____

(b) 6 marbles = ____

(c) 9 marbles = ____

3. (a) $1 × 3 = $ ____, so $3 ÷ 3 = $ ____

(b) $3 × 3 = $ ____, so $9 ÷ 3 = $ ____

(c) $2 × 3 = $ ____, so $6 ÷ 3 = $ ____

4. (a) $3\overline{)6}$ (b) $3\overline{)9}$ (c) $3\overline{)30}$

5. (a) $(6 ÷ 3)$ plus 7 = ____

(b) $(3 ÷ 3)$ minus 1 = ____

(c) $(15 ÷ 3)$ minus 3 = ____

(d) $(3 ÷ 3)$ plus 5 = ____ | 16 |

Day 3   Say the tables.

Learn these:

0 ÷ 3 = 0			
3 ÷ 3 = 1			
6 ÷ 3 = 2			
9 ÷ 3 = 3			
12 ÷ 3 = 4	12 ÷ 3 = 4		
15 ÷ 3 = 5			
18 ÷ 3 = 6	18 ÷ 3 = 6		
21 ÷ 3 = 7			
24 ÷ 3 = 8			
27 ÷ 3 = 9	27 ÷ 3 = 9		
30 ÷ 3 = 10			
33 ÷ 3 = 11	33 ÷ 3 = 11		
36 ÷ 3 = 12			

1. Count back in 3s.

(a) 12 (− 3 − 3 − 3 − 3) = _____,

so 12 ÷ 3 = _____

(b) 18 (− 3 − 3 − 3 − 3 − 3 − 3) = _____,

so 18 ÷ 3 = _____

2. (a) 9 × 3 = _____, so 27 ÷ 3 = _____

(b) 11 × 3 = _____, so 33 ÷ 3 = _____

3. How many shamrocks make…?

(a) 12 leaves = _____
(b) 27 leaves = _____
(c) 18 leaves = _____
3 leaf shamrock
(d) 33 leaves = _____

4. (a) $\frac{27}{3}$ = _____   (b) $\frac{18}{3}$ = _____

5. (a) (33 ÷ 3) + 4 = _____

(b) (12 ÷ 3) − 2 = _____

(c) (9 ÷ 3) + 3 = _____

13

Day 4   Say the tables.

Learn these:

0 ÷ 3 = 0			
3 ÷ 3 = 1			
6 ÷ 3 = 2			
9 ÷ 3 = 3			
12 ÷ 3 = 4			
15 ÷ 3 = 5			
18 ÷ 3 = 6			
21 ÷ 3 = 7	21 ÷ 3 = 7		
24 ÷ 3 = 8	24 ÷ 3 = 8		
27 ÷ 3 = 9			
30 ÷ 3 = 10			
33 ÷ 3 = 11			
36 ÷ 3 = 12	36 ÷ 3 = 12		

1. How many stools make…?

stool with 3 legs

(a) 21 legs = _____
(b) 24 legs = _____
(c) 18 legs = _____
(d) 36 legs = _____

2. Factor boxes

(a) 21 / 3 ☐   (b) 36 / 3 ☐   (c) 24 / 3 ☐

3. Fill in the gaps.

(a) 30 ÷ 3 ⇒ ☐ ÷ 2 = ☐

(b) 24 ÷ 3 ⇒ ☐ ÷ 2 = ☐

(c) 27 ÷ 3 ⇒ ☐ ÷ 3 = ☐

(d) 36 ÷ 3 ⇒ ☐ ÷ 3 = ☐

4. (a) 3⟌24 (c) 3⟌30 (e) 3⟌12

(b) 3⟌36 (d) 3⟌21

16

Do Test 17 on page 66.

43

Count in 6s

Day 1   Say the tables.

	Learn these:
$0 \div 6 = 0$	$0 \div 6 = 0$
$6 \div 6 = 1$	
$12 \div 6 = 2$	
$18 \div 6 = 3$	
$24 \div 6 = 4$	
$30 \div 6 = 5$	$30 \div 6 = 5$
$36 \div 6 = 6$	
$42 \div 6 = 7$	
$48 \div 6 = 8$	
$54 \div 6 = 9$	
$60 \div 6 = 10$	$60 \div 6 = 10$
$66 \div 6 = 11$	
$72 \div 6 = 12$	

1. (a) $0 \times 6 =$ _____, so $0 \div 6 =$ _____

   (b) $5 \times 6 =$ _____, so $30 \div 6 =$ _____

   (c) $10 \times 6 =$ _____, so $60 \div 6 =$ _____

2. **Count back in 6s.**

   $30 (- 6 - 6 - 6 - 6 - 6) =$ _____,

   so $30 \div 6 =$ _____

3.   (a)   (b)   (c)

   30   0   60

   ☐ × 6   6 × ☐   ☐ × 6

4. (a) $6 \overline{|30}$ (b) $6 \overline{|60}$ (c) $6 \overline{|0}$

5. **Complete. (Divide.)**

   (a) | 0 | ÷ | 6 | = | |

   (b) | 60 | ÷ | | = | 10 |

   (c) | | | 6 | = | 5 |

13

Day 2   Say the tables.

	Learn these:
$0 \div 6 = 0$	
$6 \div 6 = 1$	$6 \div 6 = 1$
$12 \div 6 = 2$	$12 \div 6 = 2$
$18 \div 6 = 3$	$18 \div 6 = 3$
$24 \div 6 = 4$	
$30 \div 6 = 5$	
$36 \div 6 = 6$	
$42 \div 6 = 7$	
$48 \div 6 = 8$	
$54 \div 6 = 9$	
$60 \div 6 = 10$	
$66 \div 6 = 11$	
$72 \div 6 = 12$	

1. **How many ants make…?**

   ant with 6 legs

   (a) 12 legs = _____

   (b) 18 legs = _____

   (c)   6 legs = _____

2. (a) $6 \div 6 =$ _____   (c) $12 \div 6 =$ _____

   (b) $30 \div 6 =$ _____   (d) $18 \div 6 =$ _____

3. **Factor boxes**

   (a) | 18 | |
        | 3 | |

   (b) | 12 | |
        | 6 | |

   (c) | 6 | |
        | 6 | |

4. (a) $6 \overline{|12}$ (c) $6 \overline{|18}$ (e) $6 \overline{|6}$

   (b) $6 \overline{|60}$ (d) $6 \overline{|30}$ (f) $6 \overline{|0}$

5.   (a) $12 \div 6 =$ _____

   (b) $12 \div 2 =$ _____

   (c) $18 \div 6 =$ _____

   (d) $18 \div 3 =$ _____

20

Day 3 — Say the tables.

Learn these:

0	÷	6	=	0			
6	÷	6	=	1			
12	÷	6	=	2			
18	÷	6	=	3			
24	÷	6	=	4	24 ÷ 6 = 4
30	÷	6	=	5	
36	÷	6	=	6	36 ÷ 6 = 6
42	÷	6	=	7	
48	÷	6	=	8	
54	÷	6	=	9	54 ÷ 6 = 9
60	÷	6	=	10	
66	÷	6	=	11	66 ÷ 6 = 11
72	÷	6	=	12	

1.

	(a)	(b)	(c)	(d)	(e)	(f)
÷	30	6	18	24	54	60
6	5					

2. Factor boxes

(a) 66 / 6 ☐   (b) 36 / 6 ☐   (c) 24 / 6 ☐

3. How many pizzas make…?

6 pizza slices

(a) 54 slices = ____
(b) 36 slices = ____
(c) 66 slices = ____
(d) 24 slices = ____

4. Divide by 6.

	÷ 6	
(a)	24	
(b)	66	
(c)		6
(d)	54	

16

Day 4 — Say the tables.

Learn these:

0	÷	6	=	0			
6	÷	6	=	1			
12	÷	6	=	2			
18	÷	6	=	3			
24	÷	6	=	4	
30	÷	6	=	5	
36	÷	6	=	6	
42	÷	6	=	7	42 ÷ 6 = 7
48	÷	6	=	8	48 ÷ 6 = 8
54	÷	6	=	9	
60	÷	6	=	10	
66	÷	6	=	11	
72	÷	6	=	12	72 ÷ 6 = 12

1. Complete. (Divide.)

(a) 12 ÷ 6 = ☐
(b) 42 ☐ 6 ☐
(c) ☐ ☐ 6 ☐ 12
(d) 48 ☐ ☐ 8

2. Complete.

18, 48, 72, 42, ÷ 6, 60 (with boxes a, b, c, d, e)

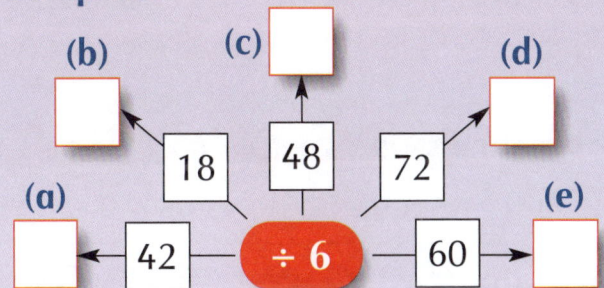

3. Write the missing numbers.

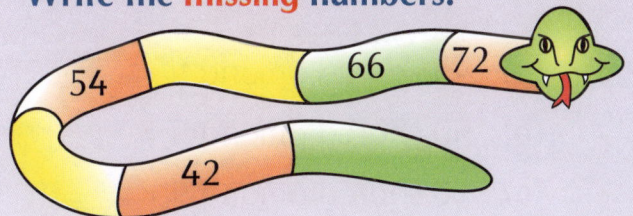

54, 66, 72, 42

4. (a) 48 divided by 6 = ____   ☐
(b) 42 shared among 6 = ____   12

Do **Test 18** on page **67**.

45

Count in 9s

Day 1 — Say the tables.

			Learn these:
0 ÷ 9 =	0		0 ÷ 9 = 0
9 ÷ 9 =	1		
18 ÷ 9 =	2		
27 ÷ 9 =	3		
36 ÷ 9 =	4		
45 ÷ 9 =	5		45 ÷ 9 = 5
54 ÷ 9 =	6		
63 ÷ 9 =	7		
72 ÷ 9 =	8		
81 ÷ 9 =	9		
90 ÷ 9 =	10		90 ÷ 9 = 10
99 ÷ 9 =	11		
108 ÷ 9 =	12		

1. (a) $\dfrac{45}{9}$ = ____   (b) $\dfrac{90}{9}$ = ____

2. Count back in 9s.

   45 (− 9 − 9 − 9 − 9 − 9) = 0,

   so 45 ÷ 9 = ____

3. (a) $9\overline{)90}$ (b) $9\overline{)0}$ (c) $9\overline{)45}$

   ____   ____   ____

4. (a) ⑤⑤⑤⑤⑤⑤⑤⑤⑤

   5 × 9 = ____, so 45 ÷ 9 = ____

   (b) ⑩⑩⑩⑩⑩⑩⑩⑩⑩

   9 × 10 = ____, so 90 ÷ 9 = ____

5. (a) 45 shared among 9 = ____

   (b) 90 shared among 9 = ____

   (c) 0 shared among 9 = ____

   (d) (90 ÷ 9) plus 4   = ____

   (e) (45 ÷ 9) minus 3   = ____

   (f) (0 ÷ 9) plus 6   = ____   **14**

Day 2 — Say the tables.

			Learn these:
0 ÷ 9 =	0		
9 ÷ 9 =	1		9 ÷ 9 = 1
18 ÷ 9 =	2		18 ÷ 9 = 2
27 ÷ 9 =	3		27 ÷ 9 = 3
36 ÷ 9 =	4		
45 ÷ 9 =	5		
54 ÷ 9 =	6		
63 ÷ 9 =	7		
72 ÷ 9 =	8		
81 ÷ 9 =	9		
90 ÷ 9 =	10		
99 ÷ 9 =	11		
108 ÷ 9 =	12		

1. (green bar of 9 dots)   (a) 9 ÷ 9 = ____

   (red bar of dots)   (b) 27 ÷ 9 = ____

   (yellow bar of dots)   (c) 18 ÷ 9 = ____

2. How many umbrellas can I buy with…?

   (umbrella priced €9)

   (a) €45 = ____

   (b) €9 = ____

   (c) €18 = ____

   (d) €27 = ____

3. (a) 1 × 9 = ____, so 9 ÷ 9 = ____

   (b) 2 × 9 = ____, so 18 ÷ 9 = ____

   (c) 3 × 9 = ____, so 27 ÷ 9 = ____

4. (a) $9\overline{)27}$ (c) $9\overline{)9}$ (e) $9\overline{)0}$

   ____   ____   ____

   (b) $9\overline{)45}$ (d) $9\overline{)18}$

   ____   ____   **15**

Day 3 — Say the tables.

Learn these:

0	÷	9	=	0
9	÷	9	=	1
18	÷	9	=	2
27	÷	9	=	3
36	÷	9	=	4
45	÷	9	=	5
54	÷	9	=	6
63	÷	9	=	7
72	÷	9	=	8
81	÷	9	=	9
90	÷	9	=	10
99	÷	9	=	11
108	÷	9	=	12

Learn these:
36 ÷ 9 = 4
54 ÷ 9 = 6
81 ÷ 9 = 9
99 ÷ 9 = 11

1. How many boxes hold…?

box with 9 chicks

(a) 36 chicks = _____
(b) 12 chicks = _____
(c) 54 chicks = _____
(d) 81 chicks = _____
(e) 99 chicks = _____

2. Write the missing numbers.

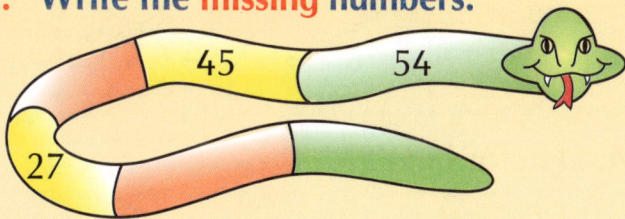

45   54
27

3.
(a) 9)54 ___   (c) 9)81 ___   (e) 9)36 ___
(b) 9)99 ___   (d) 9)27 ___   (f) 9)18 ___

4.

÷	(a) 18	(b)	(c) 81	(d)	(e) 36
9		6		11	

17

Day 4 — Say the tables.

Learn these:

0	÷	9	=	0
9	÷	9	=	1
18	÷	9	=	2
27	÷	9	=	3
36	÷	9	=	4
45	÷	9	=	5
54	÷	9	=	6
63	÷	9	=	7
72	÷	9	=	8
81	÷	9	=	9
90	÷	9	=	10
99	÷	9	=	11
108	÷	9	=	12

Learn these:
63 ÷ 9 = 7
72 ÷ 9 = 8
108 ÷ 9 = 12

1. Divide by 9.

÷ 9	
(a) 18	
(b)	3
(c) 45	
(d)	8

÷ 9	
(e) 54	
(f)	7
(g)	12
(h) 99	

2. Factor boxes

(a) 72 / 9 □   (b) 63 / 9 □   (c) 108 / 9 □

3.
(a) 9)9 ___   (c) 9)72 ___   (e) 9)18 ___
(b) 9)63 ___   (d) 9)108 ___   (f) 9)45 ___

4.
(a) 63 shared among 9 = _____
(b) 36 divided by 9 = _____
(c) 99 divided by 9 = _____
(d) (108 ÷ 9) − 4 = _____

21

Do **Test 19** on page **67**.

Revision E   Division by 3, 6 and 9

Revision 17

1. Complete.

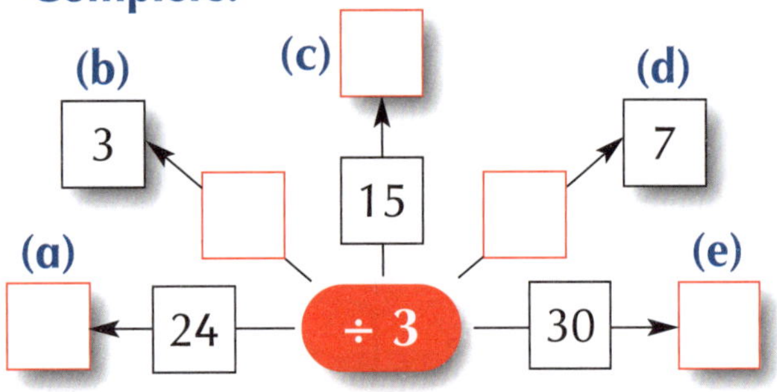

(b) 3
(c) ☐
(d) 7
15
(a) ☐
24 — ÷ 3 — 30
(e) ☐

2.
(a) (18 ÷ 3) plus 3 = ____
(b) (12 ÷ 3) add 6 = ____
(c) (27 ÷ 3) divided by 9 = ____
(d) (33 ÷ 3) multiplied by 3 = ____
(e) (30 ÷ 3) minus 9 = ____
(f) (36 ÷ 3) divided by 3 = ____

3. Match.

÷ 3	
(a) 33•	•7
(b) 9•	•0
(c) 21•	•3
(d) 0•	•11

4. How many vases hold…?

(a) 3 flowers = ____
(b) 9 flowers = ____
(c) 18 flowers = ____
(d) 27 flowers = ____

5.
(a) 3⟌3
(d) 3⟌33
(b) 3⟌12
(e) 3⟌27
(c) 3⟌18
(f) 3⟌36

25

Revision 18

1.
(a) $\frac{12}{6}$ = ____
(d) $\frac{18}{6}$ = ____
(b) $\frac{36}{6}$ = ____
(e) $\frac{48}{6}$ = ____
(c) $\frac{60}{6}$ = ____
(f) $\frac{6}{6}$ = ____

2. How many helmets can I buy with…?

€6

(a) €6 = ____
(b) €36 = ____
(c) €54 = ____
(d) €60 = ____
(e) €72 = ____
(f) €18 = ____

3. Fill in the gaps.

(a) 18 ÷ ⑥ ⇒ ☐ + ⑨ = ☐
(b) 6 ÷ ⑥ ⇒ ☐ + ⑧ = ☐
(c) 42 ÷ ⑥ ⇒ ☐ − ③ = ☐
(d) 36 ÷ ⑥ ⇒ ☐ ÷ ⑥ = ☐
(e) 72 ÷ ⑥ ⇒ ☐ ÷ ⑥ = ☐

4. Factor boxes

(a) 24 / 6 ☐
(b) 36 / 6 ☐
(c) 54 / 9 ☐

5. Complete. (Divide.)

(a)	24	÷	6	=	
(b)		÷	6	=	2
(c)	54			=	9
(d)	72		6		
(e)			6		8

25

Revision 19

1. Fill in the gaps.

(a) $\boxed{18} \div \bigcirc{9} \Rightarrow \square + \bigcirc{5} = \square$

(b) $\boxed{54} \div \bigcirc{9} \Rightarrow \square \div \bigcirc{3} = \square$

(c) $\boxed{72} \div \bigcirc{9} \Rightarrow \square - \bigcirc{6} = \square$

(d) $\boxed{81} \div \bigcirc{9} \Rightarrow \square \div \bigcirc{3} = \square$

2.

(a) $\dfrac{18}{9} = \underline{\hspace{2em}}$ (d) $\dfrac{27}{9} = \underline{\hspace{2em}}$

(b) $9\overline{)81}$ (e) $9\overline{)108}$

(c) $9\overline{)54}$ (f) $9\overline{)36}$

3. Complete.

(b) $\square$ (c) $\boxed{5}$ (d) $\boxed{9}$

$\boxed{54}$ $\square$ $\square$

(a) $\boxed{2} \leftarrow \square \leftarrow \div 9 \rightarrow \boxed{27} \rightarrow \square$ (e)

4.

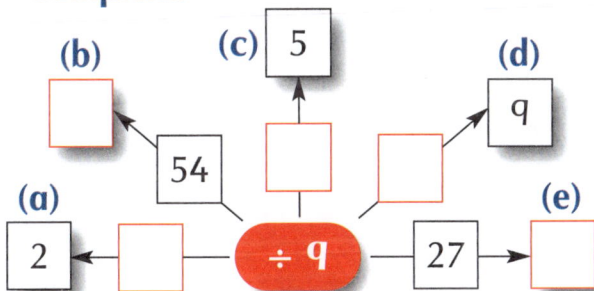

(a) $(27 \div 9)$ plus 6 $= \underline{\hspace{2em}}$

(b) $(45 \div 9)$ minus 3 $= \underline{\hspace{2em}}$

(c) $(90 \div 9)$ minus 6 $= \underline{\hspace{2em}}$

(d) 72 shared among 9 $= \underline{\hspace{2em}}$

(e) 54 divided by 9 $= \underline{\hspace{2em}}$

5. Complete. (Divide.)

(a) $63 \div 9 = \square$

(b) $27 \div \square = 3$

(c) $\square \div 9 = 5$

(d) $90 \div \square = 9$

(e) $72 \div \square = 9$

Revision 20

1.

(a) $\dfrac{24}{3} = \underline{\hspace{2em}}$ (c) $\dfrac{42}{6} = \underline{\hspace{2em}}$

(b) $\dfrac{45}{9} = \underline{\hspace{2em}}$ (d) $\dfrac{54}{9} = \underline{\hspace{2em}}$

2. $\bigcirc{>}$, $\bigcirc{<}$ or $\bigcirc{=}$

(a) $27 \div 3 \ \bigcirc \ 10 - 3$

(b) $54 \div 9 \ \bigcirc \ 18 \div 3$

(c) $48 \div 6 \ \bigcirc \ 5 \times 2$

(d) $30 \div 3 \ \bigcirc \ 60 \div 6$

(e) $72 \div 9 \ \bigcirc \ 36 \div 6$

(f) $81 \div 9 \ \bigcirc \ 66 \div 6$

3. Fill in the gaps.

(a) $\boxed{36} \ \div 6 \ \square \ \div 3 \ \square$

(b) $\boxed{54} \ \div 9 \ \square \ \div 3 \ \square$

(c) $\boxed{72} \ \div 6 \ \square \ \div 6 \ \square$

(d) $\boxed{81} \ \div 9 \ \square \ - 9 \ \square$

4. Factor boxes

(a) 60 / 6   (b) 27 / 3   (c) 54 / 6

(d) 72 / 9   (e) 18 / 3   (f) 108 / 9

5. Match. ÷ 9

(a) 99•   •4

(b) 54•   •5

(c) 45•   •11

(d) 36•   •6

(e) 27•   •3

25   25

Count in 7s

Day 1   Say the tables.

	Learn these:
$0 \div 7 = 0$	$0 \div 7 = 0$
$7 \div 7 = 1$	
$14 \div 7 = 2$	
$21 \div 7 = 3$	
$28 \div 7 = 4$	
$35 \div 7 = 5$	$35 \div 7 = 5$
$42 \div 7 = 6$	
$49 \div 7 = 7$	
$56 \div 7 = 8$	
$63 \div 7 = 9$	
$70 \div 7 = 10$	$70 \div 7 = 10$
$77 \div 7 = 11$	
$84 \div 7 = 12$	

1. (a) $5 \times 7 =$ _____

   (b) $35 \div 5 =$ _____

   (c) $35 \div 7 =$ _____

2. (a) $7\overline{)35}$ (b) $7\overline{)70}$ (c) $7\overline{)0}$

3. $10 \times 7 =$ _____, so $70 \div 7 =$ _____

4. (a) $0 \times 7 =$ _____, so $0 \div 7 =$ _____

   (b) $5 \times 7 =$ _____, so $35 \div 7 =$ _____

   (c) $10 \times 7 =$ _____, so _____ $\div 7 = 10$

5. (a) $\dfrac{70}{7} =$ _____   (b) $\dfrac{35}{7} =$ _____

6. (a) 35 shared among 5 = _____

   (b) 70 shared among 7 = _____

   (c) $(35 \div 7) + 7 =$ _____ | 15 |

Day 2   Say the tables.

	Learn these:
$0 \div 7 = 0$	
$7 \div 7 = 1$	$7 \div 7 = 1$
$14 \div 7 = 2$	$14 \div 7 = 2$
$21 \div 7 = 3$	$21 \div 7 = 3$
$28 \div 7 = 4$	
$35 \div 7 = 5$	
$42 \div 7 = 6$	
$49 \div 7 = 7$	
$56 \div 7 = 8$	
$63 \div 7 = 9$	
$70 \div 7 = 10$	
$77 \div 7 = 11$	
$84 \div 7 = 12$	

1. (a) $7 \div 7 =$ _____

   (b) $21 \div 7 =$ _____

   (c) $14 \div 7 =$ _____

2. Fill in the gaps.

   (a) $\boxed{35} \div \bigcirc{7} \Rightarrow \boxed{5} + \bigcirc{8} = \boxed{}$

   (b) $\boxed{21} \div \bigcirc{7} \Rightarrow \boxed{} - \bigcirc{1} = \boxed{}$

   (c) $\boxed{7} \div \bigcirc{7} \Rightarrow \boxed{} + \bigcirc{9} = \boxed{}$

   (d) $\boxed{14} \div \bigcirc{7} \Rightarrow \boxed{} + \bigcirc{6} = \boxed{}$

3. Factor boxes

   (a) 14 / 7   (b) 7 / 7   (c) 21 / 7

4. How many weeks in…?

   (a) 7 days = _____

   (b) 0 days = _____

   (c) 21 days = _____

   (d) 14 days = _____ | 14 |

Day 3 Say the tables.

				Learn these:
0	÷ 7	=	0	
7	÷ 7	=	1	
14	÷ 7	=	2	
21	÷ 7	=	3	
28	÷ 7	=	4	28 ÷ 7 = 4
35	÷ 7	=	5	
42	÷ 7	=	6	42 ÷ 7 = 6
49	÷ 7	=	7	
56	÷ 7	=	8	
63	÷ 7	=	9	63 ÷ 7 = 9
70	÷ 7	=	10	
77	÷ 7	=	11	77 ÷ 7 = 11
84	÷ 7	=	12	

1. (a) $9 \times 7 =$ _____, so _____ ÷ 7 = 9

   (b) $11 \times 7 =$ _____, so _____ ÷ 7 = 11

2. How many cakes have…?

   (a) 28 candles = _____

   (b) 35 candles = _____

   (c) 63 candles = _____

   (d) 42 candles = _____

   (e) 77 candles = _____

   7 candles

3. (a) 7⟌42   (c) 7⟌63   (e) 7⟌77

   (b) 7⟌35   (d) 7⟌28   (f) 7⟌70

4. (a) 28 shared among 7 = _____

   (b) 63 divided by 7 = _____

   (c) 42 shared among 7 = _____

   (d) (77 ÷ 7) plus 4 = _____

   (e) (70 ÷ 7) minus 6 = _____   18

Day 4 Say the tables.

				Learn these:
0	÷ 7	=	0	
7	÷ 7	=	1	
14	÷ 7	=	2	
21	÷ 7	=	3	
28	÷ 7	=	4	
35	÷ 7	=	5	
42	÷ 7	=	6	
49	÷ 7	=	7	49 ÷ 7 = 7
56	÷ 7	=	8	56 ÷ 7 = 8
63	÷ 7	=	9	
70	÷ 7	=	10	
77	÷ 7	=	11	
84	÷ 7	=	12	84 ÷ 7 = 12

1. (a) $8 \times 7 =$ _____, so _____ ÷ 7 = 8

   (b) $12 \times 7 =$ _____, so _____ ÷ 7 = 12

   (c) $7 \times 7 =$ _____, so _____ ÷ 7 = 7

2. How many Snow Whites for…?

   (a) 84 dwarfs = _____

   (b) 56 dwarfs = _____

   (c) 49 dwarfs = _____

   (d) 42 dwarfs = _____

   7 dwarfs

3. Factor boxes

   (a) 49 / 7 ☐   (b) 56 / 7 ☐   (c) 84 / 7 ☐

4. Complete. (Divide.)

   (a) 56 ÷ 7 = ☐

   (b) 84 ☐ 7 = ☐

   (c) ☐ ÷ 7 = 7

   (d) 28 ☐ 7 ☐   14

Do Test 20 on page 68.

Count in 11s

0 | 11 | 22 | 33 | 44

Day 1 — Say the tables.

				Learn these:
0	÷ 11	=	0	0 ÷ 11 = 0
11	÷ 11	=	1	
22	÷ 11	=	2	
33	÷ 11	=	3	
44	÷ 11	=	4	
55	÷ 11	=	5	55 ÷ 11 = 5
66	÷ 11	=	6	
77	÷ 11	=	7	
88	÷ 11	=	8	
99	÷ 11	=	9	
110	÷ 11	=	10	110 ÷ 11 = 10
121	÷ 11	=	11	
132	÷ 11	=	12	

1. (a) 5 5 5 5 5 5 5 5 5 5 5
$11 \times 5 =$ ____, so $55 \div 11 =$ ____

(b) 10 10 10 10 10 10 10 10 10 10 10
$11 \times 10 =$ ____, so $110 \div 11 =$ ____

(c) 0 0 0 0 0 0 0 0 0 0 0
$11 \times 0 =$ ____, so $0 \div 11 =$ ____

2. **Count back in 11s.**
55 (− 11 − 11 − 11 − 11 − 11) = 0,
so $55 \div 11 =$ ____

3. (a) 11|55 (b) 11|110 (c) 11|0

4. **Factor boxes**
(a) 110 / 11 (b) 55 / 5 (c) 0 / 11

5. (a) $110 \div 11 =$ ____
(b) $55 \div 11 =$ ____   12

Day 2 — Say the tables.

				Learn these:
0	÷ 11	=	0	
11	÷ 11	=	1	11 ÷ 11 = 1
22	÷ 11	=	2	22 ÷ 11 = 2
33	÷ 11	=	3	33 ÷ 11 = 3
44	÷ 11	=	4	
55	÷ 11	=	5	
66	÷ 11	=	6	
77	÷ 11	=	7	
88	÷ 11	=	8	
99	÷ 11	=	9	
110	÷ 11	=	10	
121	÷ 11	=	11	
132	÷ 11	=	12	

1. (a) $33 \div 11 =$ ____
(b) $11 \div 11 =$ ____
(c) $22 \div 11 =$ ____

2. (a) 11|22 (c) 11|33 (e) 11|55
(b) 11|110 (d) 11|11 (f) 11|0

3. **How many monsters have…?**
monster with 11 legs
(a) 33 legs = ____
(b) 22 legs = ____
(c) 11 legs = ____
(d) 55 legs = ____

4. (a) $1 \times 11 = 11$, so $11 \div 11 =$ ____
(b) $3 \times 11 =$ ____, so ____ $\div 11 = 3$
(c) $2 \times 11 =$ ____, so $22 \div 11 =$ ____

5. 33 divided by 11 = ____   17

Day 3 — Say the tables.

Learn these:

0	÷	11	=	0
11	÷	11	=	1
22	÷	11	=	2
33	÷	11	=	3
44	÷	11	=	4
55	÷	11	=	5
66	÷	11	=	6
77	÷	11	=	7
88	÷	11	=	8
99	÷	11	=	9
110	÷	11	=	10
121	÷	11	=	11
132	÷	11	=	12

Learn these:
44 ÷ 11 = 4
66 ÷ 11 = 6
99 ÷ 11 = 9
121 ÷ 11 = 11

1. (a) 11⟌66   (c) 11⟌99   (e) 11⟌44

(b) 11⟌121   (d) 11⟌33   (f) 11⟌110

2. How many caterpillars have…?

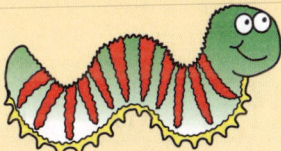

caterpillar with 11 stripes

(a) 66 stripes = ____
(b) 99 stripes = ____
(c) 44 stripes = ____
(d) 121 stripes = ____

3. Factor boxes

(a) | 44 |
    | 11 | |

(b) | 66 |
    | 11 | |

(c) | 121 |
    | 11 | |

4.

÷	(a) 44	(b) 22	(c) 66	(d) 11	(e) 99	(f) 121
11						

5. (a) (66 ÷ 11) plus 8 = ____
(b) (99 ÷ 11) minus 7 = ____   21

Day 4 — Say the tables.

Learn these:

0	÷	11	=	0
11	÷	11	=	1
22	÷	11	=	2
33	÷	11	=	3
44	÷	11	=	4
55	÷	11	=	5
66	÷	11	=	6
77	÷	11	=	7
88	÷	11	=	8
99	÷	11	=	9
110	÷	11	=	10
121	÷	11	=	11
132	÷	11	=	12

Learn these:
77 ÷ 11 = 7
88 ÷ 11 = 8
132 ÷ 11 = 12

1. (a) 7 × 11 = ____, so ____ ÷ 11 = 7
(b) 8 × 11 = ____, so ____ ÷ 11 = 8

2. Complete.

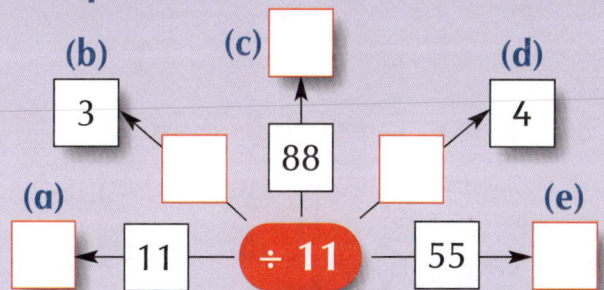

3. (a) 11⟌66   (c) 11⟌88   (e) 11⟌132

(b) 11⟌55   (d) 11⟌77   (f) 11⟌99

4. (a) ____ × 11 = 44
(b) ____ × 11 = 77
(c) ____ × 11 = 132
(d) ____ × 11 = 88
(e) ____ × 11 = 121

18

Do **Test 21** on page **68**.

Count in 12s

Day 1   Say the tables.

		Learn these:
$0 \div 12 = 0$		$0 \div 12 = 0$
$12 \div 12 = 1$		
$24 \div 12 = 2$		
$36 \div 12 = 3$		
$48 \div 12 = 4$		
$60 \div 12 = 5$		$60 \div 12 = 5$
$72 \div 12 = 6$		
$84 \div 12 = 7$		
$96 \div 12 = 8$		
$108 \div 12 = 9$		
$120 \div 12 = 10$		$120 \div 12 = 10$
$132 \div 12 = 11$		
$144 \div 12 = 12$		

1. (a) $0 \times 12 =$ _____, so $0 \div 12 =$ _____

   (b) $5 \times 12 =$ _____, so $60 \div 12 =$ _____

2. (a) $12\overline{)60}$ (b) $12\overline{)120}$ (c) $12\overline{)0}$

3. How many **cartons** hold…?

   12 eggs

   (a) 60 eggs = _____

   (b) 120 eggs = _____

   (c)   0 eggs = _____

4. (a) $\dfrac{120}{12} =$ _____   (b) $\dfrac{60}{12} =$ _____

5. Factor boxes

   (a) ☐ / 0 | 12   (b) 120 / 10 | ☐   (c) 60 / 5 | ☐

6. (a) 60 divided by 12 = _____

   (b) 120 divided by 12 = _____

   (c) 0 divided by 12 = _____

   (d) $(60 \div 12)$ minus 4 = _____

   17

Day 2   Say the tables.

		Learn these:
$0 \div 12 = 0$		
$12 \div 12 = 1$		$12 \div 12 = 1$
$24 \div 12 = 2$		$24 \div 12 = 2$
$36 \div 12 = 3$		$36 \div 12 = 3$
$48 \div 12 = 4$		
$60 \div 12 = 5$		
$72 \div 12 = 6$		
$84 \div 12 = 7$		
$96 \div 12 = 8$		
$108 \div 12 = 9$		
$120 \div 12 = 10$		
$132 \div 12 = 11$		
$144 \div 12 = 12$		

1.

   (a) $24 \div 12 =$ _____

   (b) $12 \div 12 =$ _____

   (c) $36 \div 12 =$ _____

2. (a) $12\overline{)36}$ (c) $12\overline{)24}$ (e) $12\overline{)60}$

   (b) $12\overline{)120}$ (d) $12\overline{)12}$ (f) $12\overline{)0}$

3. Fill in the gaps.

   (a) $24 \div 12 \Rightarrow$ ☐ $+ 3 =$ ☐

   (b) $12 \div 12 \Rightarrow$ ☐ $- 1 =$ ☐

   (c) $60 \div 12 \Rightarrow$ ☐ $+ 5 =$ ☐

   (d) $36 \div 12 \Rightarrow$ ☐ $- 1 =$ ☐

   (e) $0 \div 12 \Rightarrow$ ☐ $+ 8 =$ ☐

4. (a) 36 divided by 12   = _____

   (b) 24 shared among 12 = _____

   (c) $(0 \div 12)$ plus 8   = _____

   17

Day 3 — Say the tables.

Learn these:

$0 \div 12 = 0$
$12 \div 12 = 1$
$24 \div 12 = 2$
$36 \div 12 = 3$
$48 \div 12 = 4$ $48 \div 12 = 4$
$60 \div 12 = 5$
$72 \div 12 = 6$ $72 \div 12 = 6$
$84 \div 12 = 7$
$96 \div 12 = 8$
$108 \div 12 = 9$ $108 \div 12 = 9$
$120 \div 12 = 10$
$132 \div 12 = 11$ $132 \div 12 = 11$
$144 \div 12 = 12$

1. [6 6 6 6 6 6] [6 6 6 6 6 6] $6 \times 12 = 72$, so $72 \div 12 = \_\_\_$

2. **Factor boxes**

(a) 48 / 12 | ___
(b) 108 / 12 | ___
(b) 72 / ___ | 12

3. **How many flowers have…?**

flower with 12 petals

(a) 72 petals = ____
(b) 48 petals = ____
(c) 132 petals = ____
(d) 108 petals = ____
(e) 36 petals = ____

4. **Fill in the gaps.**

(a) [48] ÷12 → [4] +2 → [ ]
(b) [72] ÷12 → [ ] −3 → [ ]
(c) [108] ÷12 → [ ] +4 → [ ]
(d) [132] ÷12 → [ ] −1 → [ ]   **13**

Day 4 — Say the tables.

Learn these:

$0 \div 12 = 0$
$12 \div 12 = 1$
$24 \div 12 = 2$
$36 \div 12 = 3$
$48 \div 12 = 4$
$60 \div 12 = 5$
$72 \div 12 = 6$
$84 \div 12 = 7$ $84 \div 12 = 7$
$96 \div 12 = 8$ $96 \div 12 = 8$
$108 \div 12 = 9$
$120 \div 12 = 10$
$132 \div 12 = 11$
$144 \div 12 = 12$ $144 \div 12 = 12$

1. **How many balls can I buy with…?**

€12

(a) €84 = ____
(b) €96 = ____
(c) €72 = ____
(d) €144 = ____

2. **Complete.**

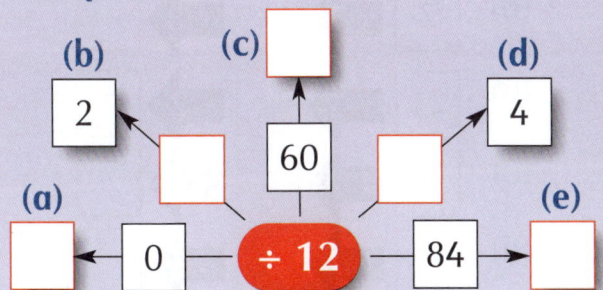

3. (a) $12\overline{)84}$ (c) $12\overline{)96}$ (e) $12\overline{)144}$

   (b) $12\overline{)72}$ (d) $12\overline{)108}$ (f) $12\overline{)60}$

4. (a) $(96 \div 12) + 2 = \_\_\_$
   (b) $(84 \div 12) - 2 = \_\_\_$ **17**

Do **Test 22** on page **69**.

Revision F Division by 7, 11 and 12

Revision 21

1. (a) $21 \div 7 =$ _____ | (c) $7 \div 7 =$ _____

(b) $0 \div 7 =$ _____ | (d) $49 \div 7 =$ _____

2. Complete

(b) 7

(c) ☐

(d) 3

(a) 2 ← ☐ ← ÷ 7 ← 35 → ☐ (e)

56

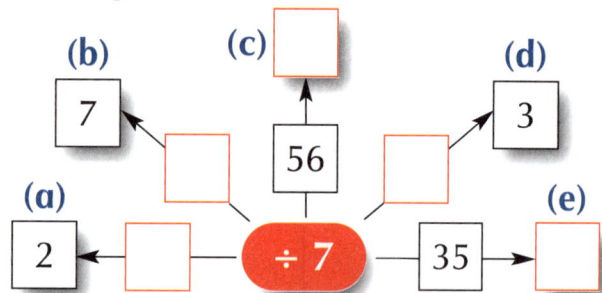

3. How many apples can I buy for…?

7c

(a) $70c =$ _____

(b) $84c =$ _____

(c) $49c =$ _____

(d) $14c =$ _____

(e) $56c =$ _____

4. Fill in the gaps.

(a) 7 ÷7 ☐ +8 ☐

(b) 21 ÷7 ☐ −2 ☐

(c) 56 ÷7 ☐ ×2 ☐

(d) 77 ÷7 ☐ −3 ☐

(e) 35 ÷7 ☐ ×4 ☐

(f) 49 ÷7 ☐ ÷7 ☐

5. (a) $7\overline{)0}$ | (c) $7\overline{)14}$ | (e) $7\overline{)42}$

_____ _____ _____

(b) $7\overline{)70}$ | (d) $7\overline{)56}$

_____ _____

25

Revision 22

1. How many tickets can I buy for…?

TICKET

Admit one Child

€11

(a) €11 = _____

(b) €33 = _____

(c) €99 = _____

(d) €110 = _____

(e) €77 = _____

2. (a) $\dfrac{99}{11} =$ _____ | (c) $\dfrac{77}{11} =$ _____

(b) $11\overline{)88}$ _____ | (d) $11\overline{)11}$ _____

3. Match.

÷ 11	
(a) 55 •	• 4
(b) 44 •	• 8
(c) 22 •	• 2
(d) 121 •	• 11
(e) 88 •	• 1
(f) 11 •	• 5

4. (a) 66 shared among 11 = _____

(b) 44 divided by 11 = _____

(c) 110 shared among 11 = _____

(d) (99 ÷ 11) plus 8 = _____

(e) (121 ÷ 11) minus 8 = _____

5. Complete. (Divide.)

(a) | 33 | ÷ | 11 | = | ☐ |

(b) | 77 | | | = | 7 |

(c) | 99 | | 11 | = | ☐ |

(d) | 88 | ÷ | | | 8 |

(e) | ☐ | | 11 | | 12 |

25

Revision 23

1. (a) $\dfrac{12}{12}$ = ____   (c) $\dfrac{36}{12}$ = ____

   (b) $\dfrac{60}{12}$ = ____   (d) $\dfrac{84}{12}$ = ____

2. **Factor boxes**

   (a) | 24 |
       | | 12 |

   (b) | | |
       | 4 | 12 |

   (c) | 72 | |
       | 6 | |

   (d) | | |
       | 8 | 12 |

   (e) | 108 | |
       | | 12 |

   (f) | 144 | |
       | | 12 |

3. **How many boxes make...?**

   (a) 12kg = ____

   (b) 36kg = ____

   (c) 84kg = ____

   (d) 24kg = ____

   (e) 108kg = ____

4. (a) $12\overline{\smash)36}$ (c) $12\overline{\smash)12}$ (e) $12\overline{\smash)48}$

   (b) $12\overline{\smash)0}$ (d) $12\overline{\smash)132}$ (f) $12\overline{\smash)60}$

5. (a) 84 shared among 12 = ____

   (b) 144 divided among 12 = ____

   (c) 72 shared among 12 = ____

   (d) 48 divided by 12 = ____

25

Revision 24

1. **Fill in the gaps.**

   (a) 35 ÷ (7) ⇒ ☐ + (7) = ☐

   (b) 88 ÷ (11) ⇒ ☐ × (2) = ☐

   (c) 48 ÷ (12) ⇒ ☐ ÷ (4) = ☐

   (d) 63 ÷ (7) ⇒ ☐ − (5) = ☐

   (e) 99 ÷ (11) ⇒ ☐ ÷ (3) = ☐

   (f) 84 ÷ (12) ⇒ ☐ × (4) = ☐

2. (a) $7\overline{\smash)49}$ (c) $12\overline{\smash)60}$ (e) $11\overline{\smash)77}$

   (b) $11\overline{\smash)108}$ (d) $12\overline{\smash)84}$ (f) $7\overline{\smash)63}$

3. (a)   (b)   (c)

   60   ☐   84
   ╱╲   ╱╲   ╱╲
   ☐ × 12   7 × 9   ☐ × 12

4. (a) 28 divided by 7 = ____

   (b) 66 divided by 11 = ____

   (c) 60 shared among 12 = ____

   (d) 99 shared among 11 = ____

   (e) 120 divided by 12 = ____

5. (a) ____ ÷ 7 = 6

   (b) ____ ÷ 11 = 7

   (c) ____ ÷ 12 = 9

   (d) (60 ÷ 12) minus 4 = ____

   (e) (49 ÷ 7) plus 8 = ____

25

Record your **scores** on page **77.**

Test 1

1.
(a)	(b)	(c)	(d)	(e)
10	5	7	9	12
× 10	× 10	× 10	× 10	× 10
___	___	___	___	___

2. (a)   0, 10, ____, ____, ____, ____, 60.

   (b)   70, 80, ____, 100, ____, 120.

   (c)   ____, 80, 90, ____, 110, 120.

3. **How many rolls can I get with…?**

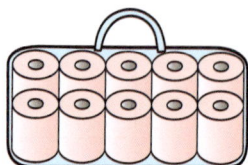

   (a)   3 packs = ____

   (b)   9 packs = ____

   (c)   7 packs = ____

   (d)   10 packs = ____

   10 rolls of toilet paper

4. **Count in 10s.**

   (a) $(10 + 10 + 10 + 10 + 10)$

      $= 10 \times$ ____

   (b) $(10 \times 7) + 3 =$ ____

   (c) $(10 \times 8) + 7 =$ ____

5. **Factor boxes**

   (a)
30	
	10

   (b)
6	10

   (c)
90	
	10

   (d)
10	10

   (e)
10	
	10

   (f)
12	10

6. (a) $(4 \times 10) + 6$ = ____

   (b) $(6 \times 10) - 8$ = ____

   (c) (9×10) plus 7   = ____

   (d) (8×10) minus 2 = ____

   25

Test 2

1. (a) $5 \times 4 =$ ____ (d) $3 \times 5 =$ ____

   (b) $5 \times 5 =$ ____ (e) $7 \times 5 =$ ____

   (c) $8 \times 5 =$ ____ (f) $12 \times 5 =$ ____

2. (a)   0, 5, ____, ____, 20, ____, 30.

   (b)   35, 40, ____, 50, ____, 60, ____.

   (c)   25, 30, ____, ____, ____, 50, 55.

3. **Complete. (Multiply.)**

   (a)
10	×	5	=	

   (b)
	×	5		15

   (c)
5		5	=	

   (d)
9			=	45

   (e)
12		5		

4.
(a)	(b)	(c)	(d)
2	5	7	9
× 5	× 10	× 5	× 5
___	___	___	___

5. **Find the cost of…**

   €5

   (a)   7 pencil cases = €____

   (b)   9 pencil cases = €____

   (c)   12 pencil cases = €____

6. (a)   ____ $\times 5 = 15$

   (b)   ____ $\times 5 = 30$

   (c)   ____ $\times 5 = 55$

   (d)   ____ $\times 5 = 0$

   25

58

Test 3

1. (a) _____ × 2 = _____

   (b) _____ × 2 = _____

2.
(a)	(b)	(c)	(d)	(e)
4	8	10	3	0
× 2	× 2	× 2	× 2	× 2
___	___	___	___	___

3. (a) 0, 2, _____, _____, 8, _____, _____.

   (b) 14, 16, _____, _____, _____, 24.

   (c) 12, 14, _____, _____, _____, 22, 24.

4. **Factor boxes**

   (a) 4 / 8   (b) 9 / 18   (c) 2 / 20

   (d) 2 3 / ___   (e) 5 / 10   (f) 7 2 / ___

5. (a) 2 = _____ × 2

   (b) 8 = _____ × 2

   (c) 16 = _____ × 2

   (d) 24 = _____ × 2

6. (a) (3 × 2) + 2 = _____

   (b) (7 × 2) + 8 = _____

   (c) (9 × 2) − 2 = _____

   (d) (10 × 2) − 6 = _____

   (e) (8 × 2) plus 3 = _____

   25

Test 4

1.
(a)	(b)	(c)	(d)	(e)
5	6	4	8	0
× 4	× 4	× 12	× 4	× 4
___	___	___	___	___

2. (a) 20 → 4 × ☐   (b) 48 → 4 × ☐   (c) 36 → 4 × ☐

3. **Match.**

× 4			× 4	
(a)	8• •28	(d)	9• •16
(b)	12• •32	(e)	6• •24
(c)	7• •48	(f)	4• •36

4. **How many legs have…?**

   (a) 3 horses = _____

   (b) 5 horses = _____

   (c) 12 horses = _____

   (d) 7 horses = _____

   (e) 9 horses = _____

   (f) 6 horses = _____

   4 legs

5. > , < or =

   (a) 4 × 4 ◯ 3 × 4

   (b) 8 × 4 ◯ 9 × 4

   (c) 4 × 7 ◯ 7 × 4

   (d) 6 × 4 ◯ 5 × 5

   (e) 9 × 4 ◯ 3 × 10

   25

Record your scores on page 76.

Test 5

1. (a) 0, 8, ____, ____, 32, ____, 48.

   (b) 56, 64, ____, 80, ____, 96.

   (c) 48, 56, ____, ____, ____, 88, 96.

2. Fill in the gaps.

   (a) $4 \times 8 \Rightarrow \Box + 3 = \Box$

   (b) $6 \times 8 \Rightarrow \Box - 6 = \Box$

   (c) $2 \times 8 \Rightarrow \Box + 8 = \Box$

   (d) $5 \times 8 \Rightarrow \Box - 4 = \Box$

   (e) $3 \times 8 \Rightarrow \Box + 5 = \Box$

   (f) $9 \times 8 \Rightarrow \Box - 8 = \Box$

3.
   (a) 64 → $8 \times \Box$

   (b) 48 → $8 \times \Box$

   (c) 8 → $8 \times \Box$

   (d) 40 → $8 \times \Box$

   (e) 32 → $8 \times \Box$

   (f) $\Box$ → 8×3

4.
   (a) $\begin{array}{r} 3 \\ \times 8 \\ \hline \end{array}$
   (b) $\begin{array}{r} 6 \\ \times 8 \\ \hline \end{array}$
   (c) $\begin{array}{r} 8 \\ \times 8 \\ \hline \end{array}$
   (d) $\begin{array}{r} 12 \\ \times 8 \\ \hline \end{array}$
   (e) $\begin{array}{r} 10 \\ \times 8 \\ \hline \end{array}$

5. (a) $8 \times$ ____ $= 64$

   (b) $9 \times 8 =$ ____

   (c) $2 \times$ ____ $= 16$

   (d) $11 \times 8 =$ ____

   (e) $12 \times 8 =$ ____

   25

Test 6

1. Complete.

   (a) $\Box$ ← 6 ← ×3

   (b) $\Box$ ← 3

   (c) 12

   (d) 36

   (e) $\Box$ → 21

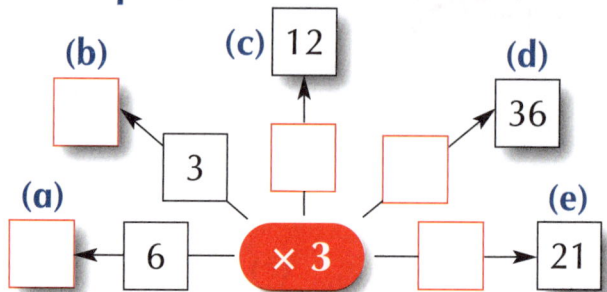

2. How many fish in…?

   fish tank

   (a) 5 tanks = ____

   (b) 7 tanks = ____

   (c) 9 tanks = ____

   (d) 8 tanks = ____

   (e) 3 tanks = ____

3. (a) $21 = 3 \times$ ____

   (b) $30 = 3 \times$ ____

   (c) $18 =$ ____ $\times 3$

   (d) $12 = 4 \times$ ____

   (e) $36 = 3 \times$ ____

4. Factor boxes

   (a) | 30 |
       |----|
       | 10 |

   (b) | 9 |
       |---|
       | 3 |

   (c) | 15 |
       |----|
       | 3 |

5. (a) 0, 3, ____, 9, ____, ____, 18.

   (b) 21, 24, ____, ____, 33, ____.

   (c) 18, 21, ____, 27, ____, 33, 36.

6. Complete. (Multiply.)

   (a) | 7 | × | 3 | = | |

   (b) | | × | 3 | | 15 |

   (c) | 8 | | | = | 24 |

   (d) | 12 | | 3 | | |

   25

Test 7

1. (a) 0, 6, ____, 18, ____, ____, 36.

   (b) 42, ____, 54, 60, ____, ____.

   (c) ____, 42, 48, ____, ____, 66, 72.

2. Complete.

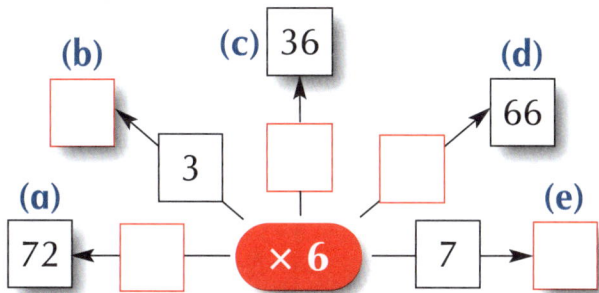

3. (a) (6 × 6) + 2 = ____

   (b) (9 × 6) − 3 = ____

   (c) (3 × 6) + 5 = ____

   (d) (12 × 6) − 3 = ____

   (e) (5 × 6) + 8 = ____

4. How many sausages make...?

   (a) 4 packs = ____

   (b) 7 packs = ____

   (c) 3 packs = ____

   (d) 0 packs = ____

5.

(a)	(b)	(c)	(d)	(e)
4	8	7	5	9
× 6	× 6	× 6	× 6	× 6
___	___	___	___	___

6. Fill in the gaps.

   (a) [6] ×6▶ [ ] +5▶ [ ]

   (b) [9] ×6▶ [ ] −3▶ [ ]

   (c) [4] ×6▶ [ ] +4▶ [ ]

25

Test 8

1. (a) 5 × 9 = 9 × ____

   (b) 9 × 2 = ____ × 9

   (c) 10 × 9 = 9 × ____

   (d) 7 × 9 = ____ × 9

   (e) 12 × 9 = 9 × ____

2. Find the cost of...

€9

   (a) 1 plant = €____

   (b) 9 plants = €____

   (c) 3 plants = €____

   (d) 7 plants = €____

   (e) 11 plants = €____

3. (a) 7 × 9 = ____

   (b) 6 × 9 = ____

   (c) 8 × 9 = ____

   (d)   5
        × 9
        ____

   (e)   9
        × 9
        ____

4. Fill in the gaps.

   (a) [3] × (9) ⇒ [ ] + (6) = [ ]

   (b) [5] × (9) ⇒ [ ] − (7) = [ ]

   (c) [12] × (9) ⇒ [ ] + (8) = [ ]

   (d) [11] × (9) ⇒ [ ] − (7) = [ ]

   (e) [7] × (9) ⇒ [ ] − (9) = [ ]

5. (>), (<) or (=)

   (a) 4 × 9 ◯ 9 × 4

   (b) 3 × 9 ◯ 9 × 4

   (c) 12 × 9 ◯ 9 × 10

   (d) 8 × 9 ◯ 7 × 4

   (e) 7 × 9 ◯ 8 × 8

25

Record your scores on page 76.

Test 9

1.

(a)	(b)	(c)	(d)	(e)
5	12	6	8	3
× 7	× 7	× 7	× 7	× 7
——	——	——	——	——

2. Find the cost of…

€7

- (a) 3 vases = €____
- (b) 0 vases = €____
- (c) 10 vases = €____
- (d) 8 vases = €____
- (e) 7 vases = €____

3. Complete. (Multiply.)

- (a) | 10 | × | 7 | = | |
- (b) | | × | 7 | | 35 |
- (c) | 7 | | 7 | = | |
- (d) | 9 | × | | | 63 |
- (e) | | | 7 | = | 56 |

4. Factor boxes

(a)
7	
49	

(b)
7	3

(c)
7	
	42

(d)
	7
63	

(e)
7	12

(f)
	7
	0

5. Match.

	× 7	
(a)	7•	•14
(b)	2•	•49
(c)	11•	•56
(d)	8•	•77

Test 10

1. Ring the correct answer.

(a)	4 × 11 =	33	44	54
(b)	11 × 7 =	75	76	77
(c)	11 × 11 =	120	121	122
(d)	2 × 11 =	0	11	22

2. Complete.

(c) 121

(b) 99

(d) 66

(a) 110

× 11

(e) 88

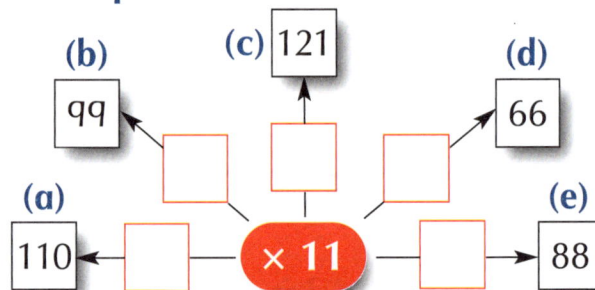

3.
- (a) 0, 11, ____, ____, 44, ____, ____.
- (b) 77, 88, ____, ____, ____, 132.

4. Match.

	× 11	
(a)	3•	• 88
(b)	4•	•110
(c)	6•	• 44
(d)	8•	• 33
(e)	10•	• 66

5. Fill in the gaps.

- (a) 3 × 11 ☐ − 3 ☐
- (b) 7 × 11 ☐ + 4 ☐
- (c) 9 × 11 ☐ − 8 ☐
- (d) 5 × 11 ☐ + 7 ☐

6.
- (a) (3 × 11) plus 4   = ____
- (b) ____ × 11   = 132
- (c) (4 × 11) minus 6 = ____
- (d) ____ × 11   = 55
- (e) (11 × 4) add 11 = ____

25

25

1. Factor boxes

(a)

6	
72	

(b)

10	12

(c)

2	
	24

(d)

12	
84	

(e)

	12
96	

(f)

5	12

2.

(a)	(b)	(c)	(d)
3	6	8	10
× 12	× 12	× 12	× 12

(e)	(f)	(g)	(h)
12	12	12	12
× 2	× 7	× 0	× 9

3. (a) 0, 12, ____, ____, 48, ____, 72.

(b) 84, ____, ____, 120, ____, ____.

4. How many buns on…?

(a) 3 trays = ____

(b) 7 trays = ____

(c) 0 trays = ____

(d) 11 trays = ____

tray of 12 buns

5. Complete. (Multiply.)

(a)

1	×	12	=	

(b)

	×	12		24

(c)

9			=	108

(d)

10			=	120

(e)

4		12		

25

1.

(a)	(b)	(c)	(d)
5	3	2	7
× 4	× 6	× 8	× 7

(e)	(f)	(g)	(h)
9	3	11	0
× 9	× 8	× 10	× 9

2. (a) 3, 6, ____, ____, 15, ____.

(b) 2, 4, ____, 8, ____, ____.

(c) 12, 16, ____, ____, ____, 32.

3. Find the cost of…

€6

(a) 3 dolls = € ____

(b) 5 dolls = € ____

(c) 4 dolls = € ____

(d) 10 dolls = € ____

4. Multiply by 12.

	× 12	
(a)	2	
(b)	10	
(c)	4	

	× 12	
(d)		60
(e)		84
(f)		36

5. >, < or =

(a) 5 × 11 ◯ 4 × 12

(b) 6 × 10 ◯ 5 × 12

(c) 2 × 7 ◯ 7 × 2

(d) 7 × 4 ◯ 11 × 3

25

Test 12

1. (a) 10)30   (c) 10)50   (e) 10)100

    (b) 10)90   (d) 10)70   (f) 10)60

2. Count back in 10s.

(a) 60, 50, ____, ____, ____, 10.

(b) 80, 70, ____, ____, ____, 30.

3. Complete. (Divide.)

(a)	20	÷	10	=	
(b)		÷	10		7
(c)	90	÷	10		
(d)		÷	10		0

4. How many bags hold…?

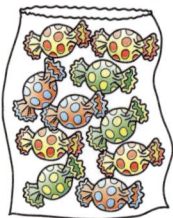

10 sweets

(a) 10 sweets = ____

(b) 80 sweets = ____

(c) 40 sweets = ____

(d) 50 sweets = ____

5. Factor boxes

(a) 40 / 10   (b) 70 / 10   (c) 80 / 10

6. Count back in 10s.

50 (− 10 − 10 − 10 − 10 − 10) = 0,

so 50 ÷ 10 = ____

7. (a) 10 ÷ 10 = ____

(b) 80 ÷ 10 = ____

(c) 40 ÷ 10 = ____

(d) 50 ÷ 10 = ____

(e) 20 ÷ 10 = ____

25

Test 13

1. (a) ____ ÷ 5 = 4

(b) ____ ÷ 5 = 6

(c) ____ ÷ 5 = 8

(d) ____ ÷ 5 = 10

2. Factor boxes

(a) 45 / 5   (b) 20 / 5   (c) 30 / 5

3. Count back in 5s.

(a) 30, 25, ____, ____, ____, 5.

(b) 60, 55, ____, 45, ____, ____.

4. Complete.

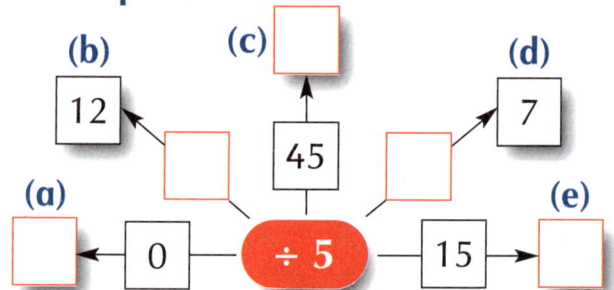

5. (a) 5)25   (c) 5)60   (e) 5)35

    (b) 5)10   (d) 5)55   (f) 5)20

6. (a) 40 ÷ 5 = ____

(b) 0 ÷ 5 = ____

(c) 15 ÷ 5 = ____

(d) 45 ÷ 5 = ____

7. Count back in 5s.

25 (− 5 − 5 − 5 − 5 − 5) = 0,

so 25 ÷ 5 = ____

25

Test 14

1. (a) $18 \div 2 = \underline{\hspace{1cm}}$ (c) $12 \div 2 = \underline{\hspace{1cm}}$

   (b) $10 \div 2 = \underline{\hspace{1cm}}$ (d) $4 \div 2 = \underline{\hspace{1cm}}$

2. **Factor boxes**

   (a)
14	
2	

   (b)
16	
2	

   (c)
8	
2	

3. (a) $2\overline{)16}$ (c) $2\overline{)22}$

   (b) $2\overline{)2}$ (d) $2\overline{)6}$

4. **How many birds have…?**

   (a) 2 wings = $\underline{\hspace{1cm}}$

   (b) 4 wings = $\underline{\hspace{1cm}}$

   (c) 10 wings = $\underline{\hspace{1cm}}$

   (d) 14 wings = $\underline{\hspace{1cm}}$

5. **Count back in 2s.**

   (a) $\underline{\hspace{1cm}}$, 12, 10, $\underline{\hspace{1cm}}$, $\underline{\hspace{1cm}}$, 4.

   (b) 24, 22, $\underline{\hspace{1cm}}$, $\underline{\hspace{1cm}}$, 16, $\underline{\hspace{1cm}}$.

6. **Fill in the gaps.**

   (a) $\boxed{20} \div \bigcirc{2} \Rightarrow \square \div \bigcirc{2} = \square$

   (b) $\boxed{8} \div \bigcirc{2} \Rightarrow \square \div \bigcirc{2} = \square$

   (c) $\boxed{24} \div \bigcirc{2} \Rightarrow \square \div \bigcirc{2} = \square$

   (d) $\boxed{16} \div \bigcirc{2} \Rightarrow \square \div \bigcirc{2} = \square$

7. **Divide by 2.**

	$\div 2$
(a) 24	
(b)	8
(c) 12	
(d) 6	

25

Test 15

1. **Count back in 4s.**

   (a) $\underline{\hspace{1cm}}$, 20, 16, $\underline{\hspace{1cm}}$, $\underline{\hspace{1cm}}$, 4.

   (b) 40, 36, $\underline{\hspace{1cm}}$, $\underline{\hspace{1cm}}$, $\underline{\hspace{1cm}}$, 20.

2. (a) $\underline{\hspace{1cm}} \div 4 = 5$

   (b) $\underline{\hspace{1cm}} \div 4 = 7$

   (c) $\underline{\hspace{1cm}} \div 4 = 6$

   (d) $\underline{\hspace{1cm}} \div 4 = 8$

3. (a) $4\overline{)36}$ (c) $4\overline{)16}$ (e) $4\overline{)44}$

   (b) $4\overline{)48}$ (d) $4\overline{)4}$ (f) $4\overline{)0}$

4. **Complete.**

   (a) $8 \leftarrow \square \leftarrow \boxed{\div 4} \leftarrow \boxed{28}$ (b) $\square \leftarrow 36$ (c) $\square \leftarrow 16$ (d) $\square \rightarrow 3$ (e) $28 \rightarrow \square$

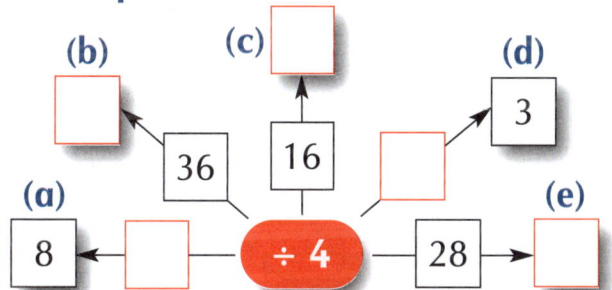

5. **How many buggies have…?**

   buggy with 4 wheels

   (a) 4 wheels = $\underline{\hspace{1cm}}$

   (b) 20 wheels = $\underline{\hspace{1cm}}$

   (c) 32 wheels = $\underline{\hspace{1cm}}$

   (d) 36 wheels = $\underline{\hspace{1cm}}$

6. **Complete. (Divide.)**

   (a)
20	$\div$	4	=	

   (b)
28	$\div$	4		

   (c)
4	$\div$		1	

   (d)
36			=	9

25

Unit 16

1. Count back in **8s**.

(a) 40, ____, ____, 16, ____, 0.

(b) 88, ____, 72, ____, ____, ____.

2. (a) ____ ÷ 8 = 8

(b) ____ ÷ 8 = 12

(c) ____ ÷ 8 = 11

(d) ____ ÷ 8 = 10

3. (a) 8⟌32   (c) 8⟌40   (e) 8⟌24

(b) 8⟌72   (d) 8⟌56   (f) 8⟌16

4. How many **teddies** can I buy for...?

(a) €8 = ____

(b) €40 = ____

(c) €24 = ____

(d) €64 = ____

€8

5. Complete.

(b) 6

(c) ☐

(d) 4

16

(a) ☐ ← 56 ← **÷ 8** → 64 → ☐ (e)

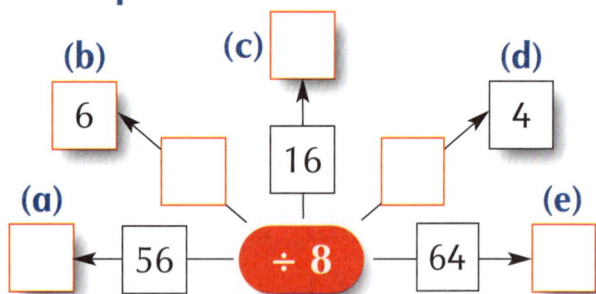

6. Fill in the gaps.

(a) 72 ÷8→ ☐ +8→ ☐

(b) 24 ÷8→ ☐ +4→ ☐

(c) 48 ÷8→ ☐ −2→ ☐

(d) 64 ÷8→ ☐ ×4→ ☐

25

Unit 17

1. (a) 3⟌30   (c) 3⟌15   (e) 3⟌24

(b) 3⟌18   (d) 3⟌21   (f) 3⟌33

2. Count back in **3s**.

(a) ____, ____, 15, 12, ____, 6.

(b) ____, 33, 30, ____, 24, ____.

3. Complete. (**Divide.**)

(a)

☐	÷	3	=	12

(b)

☐	÷	3		9

(c)

24	÷	3		☐

4. (a) (21 ÷ 3) + 6 = ____

(b) (30 ÷ 3) − 5 = ____

(c) (3 ÷ 3) + 7 = ____

5. Factor boxes

(a) 24 / 3 ☐   (b) 27 / 3 ☐   (c) 30 / 3 ☐

6. How many **boxes** hold...?

(a) 3 kittens = ____

(b) 9 kittens = ____

(c) 15 kittens = ____

(d) 24 kittens = ____

3 kittens in a box

7. (a) 27 ÷ 3 = ____

(b) 18 ÷ 3 = ____

(c) 6 ÷ 3 = ____

(d) 12 ÷ 3 = ____

25

Unit 18

1. Fill in the gaps.

(a) $12 \div 6 \;\boxed{}\; \times 4 \;\boxed{}$

(b) $18 \div 6 \;\boxed{}\; + 2 \;\boxed{}$

(c) $48 \div 6 \;\boxed{}\; \times 4 \;\boxed{}$

(d) $72 \div 6 \;\boxed{}\; \div 2 \;\boxed{}$

(e) $60 \div 6 \;\boxed{}\; \div 2 \;\boxed{}$

2.
(a) $6\overline{)36}$ (c) $6\overline{)42}$ (e) $6\overline{)54}$

(b) $6\overline{)30}$ (d) $6\overline{)66}$ (f) $6\overline{)72}$

3.
(a) $24 \div 6 =$ ____

(b) $0 \div 6 =$ ____

(c) $60 \div 6 =$ ____

(d) $54 \div 6 =$ ____

4. How many **beetles** altogether for…?

(a) 6 legs = ____

(b) 24 legs = ____

(c) 42 legs = ____

(d) 48 legs = ____

beetle with 6 legs

(e) 66 legs = ____

5.
(a) $(6 \div 6)$ plus 4 = ____

(b) $(24 \div 6)$ minus 1 = ____

(c) $(42 \div 6) + 8$ = ____

(d) $(48 \div 6) - 5$ = ____

(e) $(72 \div 6)$ plus 7 = ____

25

Unit 19

1. Divide by **9**.

	÷ 9			÷ 9
(a)	18		(d)	72	
(b)		9	(e)	54	
(c)	45		(f)		3

2. How many **boats** can I buy with…?

€9

(a) €9 = ____

(b) €18 = ____

(c) €81 = ____

(d) €27 = ____

3.
(a) $9\overline{)36}$ (c) $9\overline{)63}$ (e) $9\overline{)45}$

(b) $9\overline{)99}$ (d) $9\overline{)108}$ (f) $9\overline{)27}$

4.
(a) $\dfrac{18}{9} =$ ____ (b) $\dfrac{54}{9} =$ ____

(c) $\dfrac{99}{9} =$ ____ (d) $\dfrac{72}{9} =$ ____

3. Complete. (Divide.)

(a)	54	÷	9	=	
(b)		÷	9		3
(c)	72	÷			8
(d)		÷	9	=	11
(e)	108			=	12

25

Record your scores on page 76.

67

Unit 20

1. (a) $7\overline{)35}$ (c) $7\overline{)70}$ (e) $7\overline{)28}$

    (b) $7\overline{)49}$ (d) $7\overline{)63}$ (f) $7\overline{)42}$

2. How many books can I buy for…?

    €7 FAIRY STORIES

    (a) €7 = ____
    (b) €28 = ____
    (c) €35 = ____
    (d) €63 = ____
    (e) €56 = ____

3. (a) ____ ÷ 7 = 8
    (b) ____ ÷ 7 = 7
    (c) ____ ÷ 7 = 2
    (d) ____ ÷ 7 = 3
    (e) ____ ÷ 7 = 9

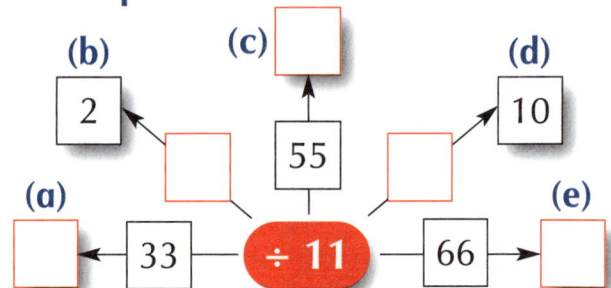

4. Factor boxes

    (a) | 14 | |
        | 7 | |

    (b) | 42 | |
        | 7 | |

    (c) | 21 | |
        | 7 | |

5. (a) $(7 ÷ 7) + 6$ = ____
    (b) $(77 ÷ 7) - 3$ = ____
    (c) $(84 ÷ 7) - 5$ = ____
    (d) $(56 ÷ 7) + 9$ = ____
    (e) $(70 ÷ 7)$ minus 3 = ____
    (f) $(49 ÷ 7)$ plus 8 = ____

    25

Unit 21

1. (a) $44 ÷ 11 =$ ____
    (b) $88 ÷ 11 =$ ____
    (c) $11 ÷ 11 =$ ____
    (d) $77 ÷ 11 =$ ____
    (e) $110 ÷ 11 =$ ____

2. Complete. (Divide.)

(a)	66	÷	11	=	
(b)	88	÷	11	
(c)	99		=	9
(d)		11	=	4
(e)	110			10

3. Complete.

    (b) 2   (c) ☐   (d) 10

    (a) ☐ ← 33   ÷ 11   55   66 → ☐ (e)

4. Factor boxes

    (a) | 99 | |
        | 11 | |

    (b) | 44 | |
        | | 4 |

    (c) | 55 | |
        | 11 | |

5. (a) $11\overline{)99}$ (b) $11\overline{)11}$ (c) $11\overline{)77}$

6. Match.

÷ 11	
(a) 33•	•2
(b) 22•	•3
(c) 66•	•9
(d) 99•	•6

    25

Unit 22

1. How many years make…?

CALENDAR

Jan	Feb	Mar
Apr	May	Jun
Jul	Aug	Sep
Oct	Nov	Dec

(a) 12 months = ____

(b) 24 months = ____

(c) 60 months = ____

(d) 72 months = ____

2. Complete.

(a) 5 ← [ ] ← ÷ 12 ← 48 → [ ] (e)

(b) [ ] ← 120

(c) [ ] ← 96

(d) [ ] → 3

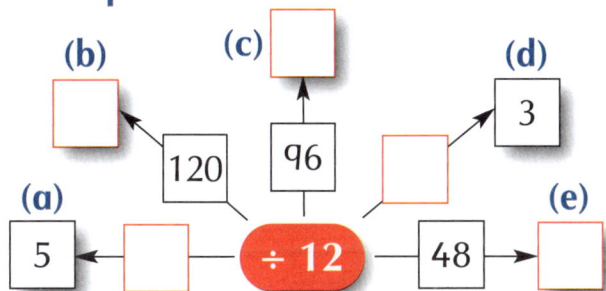

3. Count back in 12s.

(a) 60, 48, ____, ____, 12, ____.

(b) 120, 108, ____, ____, ____.

4.

(a) 12|48   (d) 12|96

(b) 12|108   (e) 12|36

(c) 12|120   (f) 12|144

5. Factor boxes

(a) | 60 | |
    | 12 | |

(b) | 120 | |
    | 12 | |

(c) | 84 | |
    | 12 | |

6.

(a) $12 \div 12 =$ ____

(b) $24 \div 12 =$ ____

(c) $60 \div 12 =$ ____

(d) $72 \div 12 =$ ____

(e) $132 \div 12 =$ ____

25

Bonus

1.

(a) 9|36   (c) 8|72   (e) 10|50

(b) 6|54   (d) 5|35   (f) 4|24

2.

÷	(a) 24	(b)	(c) 48	(d)	(e) 72
12		3		5	

3.

(a) $\dfrac{48}{6} =$ ____   (b) $\dfrac{72}{8} =$ ____

4. Fill in the gaps.

(a) 60 ÷ (12) ⇒ [ ] × (3) = [ ]

(b) 36 ÷ (6) ⇒ [ ] × (2) = [ ]

(c) 77 ÷ (7) ⇒ [ ] × (9) = [ ]

(d) 44 ÷ (11) ⇒ [ ] × (5) = [ ]

(e) 54 ÷ (9) ⇒ [ ] × (2) = [ ]

5.

(a) $(64 \div 8)$ plus 9 = ____

(b) $(32 \div 4)$ minus 3 = ____

6. Fill in the gaps.

(a) 42 ÷7 [ ] ÷2 [ ]

(b) 48 ÷6 [ ] ÷4 [ ]

(c) 63 ÷7 [ ] ÷9 [ ]

(d) 72 ÷8 [ ] ÷3 [ ]

(e) 96 ÷8 [ ] ÷4 [ ]

25

Record your **scores** on page **76**.

The Seventy Fivers   Multiplication A

Name _____   Class _____

My time _____   Score _____

	A	B	C	D	E
1.	1 × 2 = ___	2 × 6 = ___	3 × 4 = ___	0 × 3 = ___	1 × 4 = ___
2.	3 × 6 = ___	1 × 5 = ___	3 × 3 = ___	1 × 7 = ___	0 × 6 = ___
3.	4 × 3 = ___	5 × 2 = ___	2 × 7 = ___	4 × 5 = ___	7 × 2 = ___
4.	1 × 10 = ___	4 × 7 = ___	0 × 4 = ___	1 × 11 = ___	2 × 5 = ___
5.	6 × 3 = ___	2 × 11 = ___	2 × 10 = ___	2 × 3 = ___	4 × 4 = ___
6.	1 × 8 = ___	5 × 7 = ___	2 × 9 = ___	0 × 11 = ___	5 × 6 = ___
7.	7 × 10 = ___	5 × 11 = ___	6 × 4 = ___	4 × 9 = ___	2 × 8 = ___
8.	3 × 8 = ___	8 × 3 = ___	3 × 10 = ___	9 × 11 = ___	8 × 10 = ___
9.	8 × 8 = ___	7 × 6 = ___	4 × 8 = ___	6 × 5 = ___	7 × 4 = ___
10.	9 × 4 = ___	0 × 9 = ___	8 × 2 = ___	1 × 12 = ___	6 × 8 = ___
11.	6 × 11 = ___	8 × 5 = ___	7 × 7 = ___	9 × 10 = ___	8 × 6 = ___
12.	5 × 9 = ___	10 × 10 = ___	3 × 12 = ___	4 × 6 = ___	4 × 12 = ___
13.	12 × 4 = ___	11 × 7 = ___	12 × 5 = ___	9 × 5 = ___	10 × 9 = ___
14.	10 × 2 = ___	5 × 12 = ___	9 × 12 = ___	10 × 11 = ___	11 × 8 = ___
15.	8 × 12 = ___	11 × 3 = ___	6 × 9 = ___	6 × 12 = ___	9 × 7 = ___

Use the boxes below to rewrite the tables that you need to learn again.

1.					
2.					
3.					
4.					
5.					
6.					
7.					

Name _____   Class _____

My time _____   Score _____

	A	B	C	D	E
1.	2 × 2 = ___	1 × 3 = ___	0 × 5 = ___	1 × 6 = ___	3 × 3 = ___
2.	11 × 9 = ___	5 × 10 = ___	3 × 11 = ___	0 × 2 = ___	3 × 5 = ___
3.	7 × 3 = ___	0 × 10 = ___	5 × 3 = ___	1 × 9 = ___	10 × 4 = ___
4.	0 × 7 = ___	4 × 2 = ___	3 × 9 = ___	4 × 10 = ___	6 × 2 = ___
5.	4 × 11 = ___	0 × 8 = ___	3 × 7 = ___	6 × 6 = ___	2 × 4 = ___
6.	11 × 2 = ___	5 × 5 = ___	5 × 4 = ___	2 × 12 = ___	0 × 12 = ___
7.	7 × 7 = ___	6 × 7 = ___	7 × 11 = ___	9 × 2 = ___	7 × 5 = ___
8.	10 × 5 = ___	10 × 6 = ___	10 × 8 = ___	8 × 7 = ___	6 × 6 = ___
9.	4 × 9 = ___	11 × 5 = ___	9 × 3 = ___	6 × 9 = ___	5 × 8 = ___
10.	9 × 9 = ___	7 × 6 = ___	6 × 10 = ___	11 × 4 = ___	6 × 7 = ___
11.	11 × 6 = ___	8 × 4 = ___	7 × 9 = ___	9 × 5 = ___	7 × 8 = ___
12.	9 × 4 = ___	6 × 5 = ___	9 × 11 = ___	12 × 7 = ___	10 × 3 = ___
13.	12 × 2 = ___	8 × 7 = ___	12 × 8 = ___	8 × 9 = ___	12 × 10 = ___
14.	9 × 8 = ___	8 × 11 = ___	10 × 12 = ___	9 × 6 = ___	9 × 8 = ___
15.	12 × 3 = ___	7 × 12 = ___	11 × 10 = ___	10 × 10 = ___	12 × 6 = ___

Use the boxes below to rewrite the tables that you need to learn again.

1.					
2.					
3.					
4.					
5.					
6.					
7.					

The Seventy Fivers   Division C

Name _____   Class _____

My time _____   Score _____

	A	B	C	D	E
1.	2 ÷ 2 = ___	20 ÷ 5 = ___	6 ÷ 3 = ___	7 ÷ 7 = ___	15 ÷ 5 = ___
2.	8 ÷ 4 = ___	9 ÷ 9 = ___	4 ÷ 2 = ___	12 ÷ 12 = ___	30 ÷ 6 = ___
3.	6 ÷ 6 = ___	9 ÷ 3 = ___	14 ÷ 7 = ___	4 ÷ 4 = ___	8 ÷ 2 = ___
4.	12 ÷ 2 = ___	27 ÷ 9 = ___	18 ÷ 6 = ___	15 ÷ 3 = ___	10 ÷ 10 = ___
5.	40 ÷ 5 = ___	21 ÷ 7 = ___	10 ÷ 5 = ___	8 ÷ 8 = ___	12 ÷ 4 = ___
6.	18 ÷ 3 = ___	16 ÷ 2 = ___	30 ÷ 10 = ___	22 ÷ 11 = ___	36 ÷ 9 = ___
7.	60 ÷ 6 = ___	32 ÷ 8 = ___	49 ÷ 7 = ___	45 ÷ 5 = ___	22 ÷ 2 = ___
8.	40 ÷ 4 = ___	45 ÷ 9 = ___	36 ÷ 6 = ___	48 ÷ 12 = ___	50 ÷ 10 = ___
9.	27 ÷ 3 = ___	55 ÷ 5 = ___	40 ÷ 8 = ___	11 ÷ 11 = ___	66 ÷ 6 = ___
10.	33 ÷ 11 = ___	24 ÷ 4 = ___	44 ÷ 4 = ___	56 ÷ 7 = ___	90 ÷ 9 = ___
11.	36 ÷ 4 = ___	70 ÷ 10 = ___	36 ÷ 3 = ___	63 ÷ 9 = ___	63 ÷ 7 = ___
12.	42 ÷ 7 = ___	20 ÷ 4 = ___	80 ÷ 8 = ___	56 ÷ 8 = ___	72 ÷ 12 = ___
13.	80 ÷ 10 = ___	64 ÷ 8 = ___	96 ÷ 12 = ___	35 ÷ 5 = ___	66 ÷ 11 = ___
14.	54 ÷ 6 = ___	120 ÷ 12 = ___	48 ÷ 6 = ___	48 ÷ 4 = ___	99 ÷ 11 = ___
15.	100 ÷ 10 = ___	108 ÷ 9 = ___	110 ÷ 11 = ___	96 ÷ 8 = ___	144 ÷ 12 = ___

Use the boxes below to rewrite the tables that you need to learn again.

1.					
2.					
3.					
4.					
5.					
6.					
7.					

The Seventy Fivers Division D

Name _____   Class _____

My time _____   Score _____

	A	B	C	D	E
1.	$3 \div 3 =$ ___	$6 \div 2 =$ ___	$5 \div 5 =$ ___	$20 \div 10 =$ ___	$16 \div 8 =$ ___
2.	$24 \div 12 =$ ___	$18 \div 9 =$ ___	$45 \div 11 =$ ___	$12 \div 3 =$ ___	$10 \div 2 =$ ___
3.	$6 \div 6 =$ ___	$25 \div 5 =$ ___	$30 \div 3 =$ ___	$20 \div 2 =$ ___	$16 \div 4 =$ ___
4.	$14 \div 2 =$ ___	$60 \div 10 =$ ___	$24 \div 6 =$ ___	$12 \div 6 =$ ___	$50 \div 5 =$ ___
5.	$40 \div 10 =$ ___	$21 \div 3 =$ ___	$24 \div 4 =$ ___	$18 \div 2 =$ ___	$24 \div 8 =$ ___
6.	$30 \div 5 =$ ___	$28 \div 7 =$ ___	$70 \div 7 =$ ___	$27 \div 3 =$ ___	$33 \div 3 =$ ___
7.	$55 \div 11 =$ ___	$36 \div 12 =$ ___	$24 \div 3 =$ ___	$28 \div 4 =$ ___	$35 \div 7 =$ ___
8.	$15 \div 3 =$ ___	$88 \div 8 =$ ___	$36 \div 6 =$ ___	$90 \div 10 =$ ___	$63 \div 9 =$ ___
9.	$24 \div 2 =$ ___	$77 \div 7 =$ ___	$32 \div 4 =$ ___	$45 \div 5 =$ ___	$54 \div 6 =$ ___
10.	$60 \div 12 =$ ___	$48 \div 8 =$ ___	$36 \div 9 =$ ___	$77 \div 11 =$ ___	$60 \div 5 =$ ___
11.	$42 \div 6 =$ ___	$70 \div 10 =$ ___	$54 \div 9 =$ ___	$32 \div 8 =$ ___	$48 \div 6 =$ ___
12.	$49 \div 7 =$ ___	$72 \div 9 =$ ___	$63 \div 7 =$ ___	$84 \div 12 =$ ___	$72 \div 8 =$ ___
13.	$81 \div 9 =$ ___	$54 \div 6 =$ ___	$48 \div 12 =$ ___	$56 \div 8 =$ ___	$108 \div 12 =$ ___
14.	$56 \div 7 =$ ___	$84 \div 7 =$ ___	$120 \div 10 =$ ___	$72 \div 6 =$ ___	$36 \div 4 =$ ___
15.	$108 \div 9 =$ ___	$120 \div 12 =$ ___	$108 \div 12 =$ ___	$144 \div 12 =$ ___	$110 \div 11 =$ ___

Use the boxes below to rewrite the tables that you need to learn again.

1					
2					
3					
4					
5					
6					
7					

Name _____   Class _____

My time _____   Score _____

	A	B	C	D	E
1.	10 ÷ 2 = ___	6 × 2 = ___	9 ÷ 9 = ___	3 × 5 = ___	18 ÷ 9 = ___
2.	4 × 3 = ___	9 ÷ 9 = ___	1 × 8 = ___	30 ÷ 6 = ___	2 × 4 = ___
3.	14 ÷ 7 = ___	7 × 10 = ___	16 ÷ 4 = ___	0 × 8 = ___	9 ÷ 3 = ___
4.	3 × 9 = ___	18 ÷ 6 = ___	7 × 5 = ___	14 ÷ 2 = ___	2 × 7 = ___
5.	27 ÷ 3 = ___	1 × 12 = ___	24 ÷ 6 = ___	7 × 5 = ___	15 ÷ 5 = ___
6.	3 × 8 = ___	36 ÷ 9 = ___	0 × 11 = ___	48 ÷ 12 = ___	8 × 3 = ___
7.	36 ÷ 9 = ___	7 × 7 = ___	45 ÷ 5 = ___	12 × 2 = ___	21 ÷ 7 = ___
8.	5 × 6 = ___	40 ÷ 8 = ___	4 × 9 = ___	24 ÷ 3 = ___	6 × 8 = ___
9.	27 ÷ 9 = ___	9 × 5 = ___	40 ÷ 10 = ___	10 × 10 = ___	45 ÷ 9 = ___
10.	9 × 7 = ___	70 ÷ 10 = ___	9 × 6 = ___	36 ÷ 6 = ___	8 × 9 = ___
11.	25 ÷ 5 = ___	12 × 4 = ___	54 ÷ 9 = ___	11 × 2 = ___	96 ÷ 8 = ___
12.	9 × 6 = ___	44 ÷ 11 = ___	11 × 10 = ___	63 ÷ 7 = ___	9 × 10 = ___
13.	72 ÷ 8 = ___	10 × 11 = ___	64 ÷ 8 = ___	11 × 9 = ___	84 ÷ 12 = ___
14.	9 × 8 = ___	56 ÷ 7 = ___	7 × 8 = ___	72 ÷ 9 = ___	12 × 4 = ___
15.	48 ÷ 12 = ___	11 × 11 = ___	96 ÷ 12 = ___	9 × 9 = ___	100 ÷ 10 = ___

Use the boxes below to rewrite the tables that you need to learn again.

1.					
2.					
3.					
4.					
5.					
6.					
7.					

The Seventy Fivers Multiplication / Division F

Name _____ Class _____

My time _____ Score _____

	A	B	C	D	E
1.	9 ÷ 3 = ___	3 × 4 = ___	10 ÷ 5 = ___	7 × 2 = ___	16 ÷ 4 = ___
2.	1 × 6 = ___	8 ÷ 2 = ___	4 × 5 = ___	18 ÷ 6 = ___	6 × 3 = ___
3.	21 ÷ 7 = ___	5 × 7 = ___	18 ÷ 9 = ___	2 × 9 = ___	24 ÷ 8 = ___
4.	3 × 8 = ___	40 ÷ 10 = ___	5 × 10 = ___	66 ÷ 11 = ___	3 × 12 = ___
5.	24 ÷ 3 = ___	4 × 11 = ___	28 ÷ 4 = ___	5 × 5 = ___	45 ÷ 5 = ___
6.	5 × 4 = ___	48 ÷ 6 = ___	7 × 3 = ___	35 ÷ 7 = ___	9 × 2 = ___
7.	40 ÷ 8 = ___	4 × 9 = ___	54 ÷ 9 = ___	6 × 8 = ___	60 ÷ 12 = ___
8.	4 × 7 = ___	70 ÷ 10 = ___	11 × 2 = ___	55 ÷ 11 = ___	6 × 6 = ___
9.	36 ÷ 4 = ___	3 × 12 = ___	49 ÷ 7 = ___	8 × 10 = ___	72 ÷ 9 = ___
10.	9 × 11 = ___	33 ÷ 3 = ___	6 × 4 = ___	56 ÷ 8 = ___	9 × 5 = ___
11.	55 ÷ 5 = ___	8 × 7 = ___	24 ÷ 2 = ___	12 × 6 = ___	54 ÷ 6 = ___
12.	8 × 8 = ___	56 ÷ 7 = ___	9 × 6 = ___	81 ÷ 9 = ___	10 × 2 = ___
13.	72 ÷ 12 = ___	9 × 9 = ___	72 ÷ 8 = ___	7 × 12 = ___	28 ÷ 4 = ___
14.	9 × 7 = ___	99 ÷ 11 = ___	10 × 10 = ___	60 ÷ 12 = ___	8 × 7 = ___
15.	108 ÷ 9 = ___	11 × 9 = ___	96 ÷ 12 = ___	12 × 8 = ___	63 ÷ 7 = ___

Use the boxes below to rewrite the tables that you need to learn again.

1.					
2.					
3.					
4.					
5.					
6.					
7.					

Test Scores

Pupil's name: Class:

	MULTIPLICATION												DIVISION											
	Test 1	Test 2	Test 3	Test 4	Test 5	Test 6	Test 7	Test 8	Test 9	Test 10	Test 11	Bonus	Test 12	Test 13	Test 14	Test 15	Test 16	Test 17	Test 18	Test 19	Test 20	Test 21	Test 22	Bonus
25.																								
24.																								
23.																								
22.																								
21.																								
20.																								
19.																								
18.																								
17.																								
16.																								
15.																								
14.																								
13.																								
12.																								
11.																								
10.																								
9.																								
8.																								
7.																								
6.																								
5.																								
4.																								
3.																								
2.																								
1.																								

Total: /100   Total: /100   Total: /100   Total: /100   Total: /100   Total: /100

Make a bar graph of your scores.

Score yourself out of 25. After each group of four tests, score yourself out of 100.

Revision Scores

Pupil's name: _____ Class: _____

	Revision A				Revision B				Revision C				Revision D				Revision E				Revision F			
	Revision 1	Revision 2	Revision 3	Revision 4	Revision 5	Revision 6	Revision 7	Revision 8	Revision 9	Revision 10	Revision 11	Revision 12	Revision 13	Revision 14	Revision 15	Revision 16	Revision 17	Revision 18	Revision 19	Revision 20	Revision 21	Revision 22	Revision 23	Revision 24
25.																								
24.																								
23.																								
22.																								
21.																								
20.																								
19.																								
18.																								
17.																								
16.																								
15.																								
14.																								
13.																								
12.																								
11.																								
10.																								
9.																								
8.																								
7.																								
6.																								
5.																								
4.																								
3.																								
2.																								
1.																								

Total: ___/100 Total: ___/100 Total: ___/100 Total: ___/100 Total: ___/100 Total: ___/100

Make a bar graph of your scores.
Score yourself out of 25. After each revision section, score yourself out of 100.

77